Edward Nevin.

An impression of his life, times and legacy to mark the centenary of his birth.

AF879629

A Memoir by Michael Nevin

Triquetra Publishing, Edinburgh, 2024

To Caroline

"Good times never seemed so good"

Contents

1 The Early Years, 1925 to 1947

My father was born on February 5th 1925 in the maritime town of Pembroke Dock in south-west Wales, the fourth and last child of Mary Helen Nevin, née Fahey, and her husband, William Thomas Nevin.

William was a veteran of the Great War who had been invalided back to Wales after being gassed at the Battle of the Somme in 1916, but happily had recovered sufficiently to marry in 1917.

The Newly Weds, 1917

A faded photograph from 1917 shows my grandfather in British Army uniform shortly after his marriage. On his right as we look at the photograph is his new bride and on his left his mother Honora Nevin née Mullins. My father described Honora as "a saint." She gave birth to nine children, of whom four died in infancy or childhood, so must have felt her prayers had been answered when her son William came home from the Battle of the Somme (1916), in which more than 300,000 British, French and German soldiers died.

In 1918 their first daughter, Doreen, was born, followed by another daughter, Eileen, in 1920; a son, Bernard, in 1921; and finally my father in 1925.

However, his birth was not an occasion of unalloyed joy.

My grandmother's father was an Irishman by the name of Edward Fahey, a professional soldier who served as a Gunner in the Royal Horse Artillery. The regiment was deployed to India around the year 1890, where he met and married his wife Gertrude and where my grandmother was born in 1895. In 1899, the regiment had been redeployed to Natal in South Africa, where there were growing tensions with the Boers, leading to the outbreak of the Boer War. The British force in which Gunner Fahey served was defeated by the Boers at the Battle of Ladysmith and forced to fall back into the town of Ladysmith where they were besieged for several months, losing many more men during the siege to dysentery, typhoid and other diseases.

The siege was eventually lifted by a British relief column under Sir Redvers Buller which marched up from the Cape and eventually broke through the Boer lines to enter the town on St David's Day 1900. However, the tribulations of the siege had rendered Gunner Fahey unfit for active service and he was invalided out of the Army, never to serve again.

Some two years later, he received a letter from his old commanding officer, one Major Goulborn, an officer of the old school with genuine concern for the welfare of the men under his command, later promoted to Colonel and awarded the DSO. Dated April 2nd 1902, his letter reads as follows:

> "*Gunner Fahey,*
>
> *I am very sorry to hear that you have been invalided out of the service. I shall be very glad to assist you to get a place if I can and happy to be able to state that I believe you to be honest, sober and trustworthy, and by no means a bad cook. Although during the Siege of Ladysmith the fare was not very appetizing or varied, still the way you roasted the horse and cooked the mule tongues was worthy of great praise, and I always think that the good health we all enjoyed during that time was greatly due to the way you carried out your culinary duties.*"

Perhaps inspired by this praise for his cooking, after leaving the army Edward Fahey ran a fish-and-chip shop in Pembroke Dock, but his health never fully recovered and he died at the age of fifty-five on February 4th 1925. My father was born on February 5th. Thus, in less than forty-eight hours, my grandmother had lost her father and gained a son.

Given the unfortunate co-incidence of his birth with the death of his maternal grandfather, it was perhaps not surprising that my father was given his Christian name. To maintain family equilibrium, his second name was that of his surviving grandfather, Thomas Nevin.

ThUs it was that Edward Thomas Nevin embarked on the great adventure of life.

****

Unbeknownst to his parents, it proved not to be the best of times to enter the world. The family was about to be overwhelmed by shapeless forces over which they had no control that would reduce them to penury.

Following the Conservative Party victory at the 1924 General Election, Winston Churchill had been appointed Chancellor of the Exchequer, a post he held until 1929. He proved to be by some margin the worst British Chancellor of the 20th century. Churchill had no knowledge of basic economics, having considerable difficulty in managing his own financial affairs[i], and no mastery of his Treasury brief. This might not have mattered had he applied his considerable intelligence and energies to undertake some rudimentary study of the subject, but the reality was that he had very little interest in it. His real interest lay in military, defence and foreign policy. The result was that he was little more than a puppet of his Treasury civil servants and the Bank of England under its long-serving Governor, Montagu Norman.

The Treasury Orthodoxy of the day advocated a return to normalcy after the turbulence of the First World War, the Great Influenza Epidemic of 1918–1919, and the severe recession of 1920-1921. The Treasury and Bank advocated that Sterling should return to the Gold Standard at its pre-war rate – when a Guinea (twenty-one shillings) weighed approximately a quarter ounce of gold, in order to restore confidence in the stability of money. Under the Gold Standard, the Bank of England guaranteed to convert banknotes into gold at this fixed rate, which implied a rate of exchange against the American dollar of £1 = US $4.86.

On the face of it, this policy was not without its merits. However, it had one fatal flaw, pointed out by a young Cambridge economist of rising repute by the name of John Maynard Keynes.

Keynes had made his name with his 1919 book *The Economic Consequences of the Peace*, a devastating critique of the Treaty of Versailles that had brought the First World War to a close. Keynes' thesis was that the terms of the treaty were so harsh that they could not possibly be enforced because Germany did not have the means to pay the reparations demanded by the victorious allies. The result, he predicted, would be ongoing resentment within Germany and further trouble between Germany and the victorious allied powers.

Keynes's predictions were borne out by subsequent events. Twenty years later, another war was to break out between Germany and the allied powers. Churchill's guiding principles, "in war: Resolution; in defeat: Defiance; in victory: Magnanimity" proved a sounder basis for an enduring peace than the total subjugation of a defeated enemy, but these principles were only applied after the Second World War.

In 1925, it was Churchill himself whom Keynes had in his sights in *The Economic Consequences of Mr Churchill.* Or rather, not Churchill personally, but the experts who advised him. Keynes's central concern was that the rate of exchange at which Sterling returned to the Gold Standard was far too high, by at least ten per cent. He wrote that,

> *"The policy of improving the foreign-exchange value of sterling up to its pre-war value in gold from being about ten per cent below it means that, whenever we sell anything abroad, either the foreign buyer has to pay ten per cent more in his money or we have to accept ten per cent less in our money. That is to say, we have to reduce our sterling prices, for coal or iron or shipping freights or whatever it may be, by ten per cent in order to be on a competitive level."*[ii]

The overvalued exchange rate could only by maintained if British interest rates remained high enough to persuade foreign investors to hold Sterling. However, while high interest rates might benefit City financiers, they would constrain investment in industry and construction. At the same time downward pressure would be exerted on wages – "Mr. Churchill's policy of improving the exchange rate by ten per cent was, sooner or later, a policy of reducing every one's wages by two shillings in the £" wrote Keynes.

Together, these factors would, he predicted, drive the British economy into a severe recession. This would occur, he wrote,

> *"partly, perhaps, because he (Churchill) has no instinctive judgement to prevent him from making mistakes; partly because, lacking this instinctive judgement, he was deafened by the clamorous voices of conventional finance; and, most of all, because he was gravely misled by his experts."*

Once again, as at Versailles, Keynes proved accurate in his forecasts. The attempt by mine owners to cut the wages of the coal miners precipitated a General Strike in May 1926 when railwaymen, dockers, steel workers and others came out in sympathy with the miners. Although the General Strike lasted only nine days, the miners continued to strike for several months thereafter until eventually they returned to work on longer hours and lower pay.

****

Times were hard in Pembroke Dock too.

After he had been demobilised at the end of the First World War, my grandfather had returned to his old job at the Royal Naval Dockyard. Then, in 1926, as part of the economies introduced by the British Government following the return to Gold, the Naval Dockyard was closed, with a devastating impact on hundreds of families in Pembroke Dock whose main breadwinner was thrown out of work. The options open to William Nevin, with six mouths to feed including a new baby, were few. He was fortunate to secure a job with the town corporation as a dustman, though the wages paid for working on the municipal dustcarts were far lower than they had been in the Naval Dockyard.

****

I never knew William's father Thomas Nevin, as he died ten years or so before I was born. However, the stories passed down about him do not suggest a particularly warm figure, and the impression I got from my father was that his Sunday visits to his grandfather's house filled him with dread. However, family loyalty precludes me from condemning old Thomas Nevin unheard, and I would make the following points in his favour.

The first is that he himself did not have an easy journey through life. He was born in County Roscommon in south-west Ireland in the mid-nineteenth century, a child of the Great Famine. This was the very difficult period in Ireland when a million lives were claimed by starvation following the failure of successive potato harvests, and County Roscommon was one of the worst affected areas. Thomas escaped the fate of many other children by joining the British Army as a drummer boy at the age of twelve. He remained loyal to his regiment, the Worcestershires, naming a house he later acquired in Pembroke Dock after it. The Worcestershire Regiment gave Thomas Nevin not just a livelihood but a life. The pay might have been miserly, but at least he had a bed for the night and regular rations at a time when the spectre of famine still haunted those who remained in Ireland.

Loyalty was his one great virtue. He was loyal not only to his regiment, but also to his country, to whose defence he dedicated his career and for whose defence, at the hour of its maximum danger in 1914 his surviving sons volunteered, prepared, if the fates decreed, to make the ultimate sacrifice.

He was loyal to his Church and his faith. He was loyal, above all, to his family. In photographs he commissioned to record the occasion of his Golden Wedding with his wife Honora in August 1928, he is positioned centre stage, represented as a benevolent *Pater Familias* standing protectively over his grandchildren.

The Golden Wedding, 1928

Thomas and Honora Nevin with family members on the occasion of their Golden Wedding in August 1928. My father is the little boy first on the left as we view the photo.

His grandchildren, my father included, may not have seen their grandfather as a benign patriarch, regarding him with a measure of fear as an autocrat whose word was law, and whose law could be arbitrary. Indeed, one suspects that the reason my father described his grandmother, Thomas's wife Honora, as a saint is because he had an inkling of what she had to put up with over fifty-six years of married life. Nevertheless, through all the ups and downs, their marriage survived, for better, for worse; for richer, for poorer; in sickness and in health.

The Golden Wedding, 1928 : A Trip to the Beach

Another photo taken later on the day of their Golden Wedding depicts Thomas and Honora centre stage at Freshwater West, where they treated their grandchildren to a trip to the beach. The children are lined up in good order in the front row, while centre stage in the back row, just behind Thomas and Honora, stands the parish priest who has joined the expedition, doubtless for the children's moral betterment. The children look suitably glum.

It is easy to judge the conduct of those brought up in the nineteenth century by the standards of the twenty-first. Back then, there was no Welfare State and little government support if someone fell ill or became unemployed, or, biggest disaster of all, if the family breadwinner were to die. Only other family members stood between a child who had lost a father and destitution. So if a grandfather said, "Don't ask questions – just do as I say", a recalcitrant child would be well advised to remain silent and follow instructions. Whatever faults he may have had, during the depths of the Great Depression old Thomas Nevin made sure that his children were properly clothed, as evidenced by his Golden Wedding photos, that they always had food on the table, shoes, books and uniforms for school.

The Nevin family survived the Great Depression, and things began to look up in 1930 when William secured a job with the Ministry of Works. There is a photo of the family from the early Thirties which shows William back in charge, with no sign of father Thomas, and everyone looking a lot happier and more relaxed.

There's the grandmother, Honora – she passed away in 1934, so I would date this photo around 1931 or 1932. There's my grandfather, William, looking quite dapper in a Panama hat, my grandmother smiling happily; Uncle Bernie with his grandmother's hands on his shoulders; next to him, my father, with Auntie Eileen behind him and Auntie Doreen next to Eileen. My father is not wearing spectacles in this early photo; he was later to lose sight in one eye as a consequence of a childhood illness.

"Happy Days are Here Again": **The Nevin Family, c. 1932**

It's a much more cheerful family photo than those commemorating the Golden Wedding, with William back in work and earning a good living.

However, this period of peace and tranquillity soon came to an end. In September 1939 the Second World War broke out.

Pembroke Dock had the unique honour of being the only town in Britain at that time to be a home to all three of the armed services – the Royal Navy, the Army, and the youngest branch, the Royal Air Force, which was stationed there from the late Twenties.

The fact that Pembroke Dock was a base to all three services meant that it was a prime target for the Luftwaffe. In 1940 and 1941 the town was subject to a sustained blitz. It was the most heavily bombed town relative to its population in the whole of Great Britain. Most of Britain's anti-aircraft defences were concentrated in the south-east of England in order to protect London. Pembroke Dock was left more or less defenceless, so the bombers came over night after night. It must have been quite a terrifying ordeal for William Nevin and his family, huddled in their cellar in Upper Meyrick Street, not knowing whether one of the bombs had their name on it.

Fortunately, none did.

However, the Luftwaffe did score a number of successes. In August 1940, oil tanks at Llanreath were hit and thirty-three million gallons of oil spilled out, causing a huge fire – the greatest conflagration seen in Britain since the Great Fire of London in 1666. It took three weeks to put it out. Firemen were drafted in from the whole of Wales to try and put out the blaze. Five Cardiff firefighters lost their lives. Many more firemen suffered serious injuries when hot oil spilt onto their skin and into their eyes. While that fire was still blazing in September 1940, Pembroke Dock's community centre, the Temperance Hall, was hit by another bomb. As there was no money to restore it during the war, it remained a shell.

In the Summer of 1941, my father left school at the age of sixteen to work with the Ministry of Aircraft Production in Harrogate, which, one suspects, was a considerably safer location than Pembroke Dock. Two years later, aged eighteen, he joined the Army proper as a Private in the Corps of the Royal Electrical and Mechanical Engineers (REME), responsible for the maintenance and repair of military equipment. By the end of the war, he had been promoted to the rank of Sergeant in the REME.

The Squaddie, 1943

While he was being demobilised in the summer of 1946, he rejoined a local dance band in Pembroke Dock with which he had played before the War, as he recollected in 1983 in an unpublished family memoir, *Diary of a Lifetime*.[iii]

> *"In late July 1946 I returned to Pembroke Dock on demobilisation from the Army after three years' service. I had been given a Class B release, which means I had been released somewhat earlier than my demobilisation number would normally have*

involved because I had secured a place in a university – in my case, the University College of Wales, Aberystwyth – under a revolutionary scheme called the Further Education and Training Scheme, devised for servicemen, (which) decreed that any ex-serviceman who had the qualifications – broadly speaking, who could read or write – was entitled to admission to a university and, furthermore, all universities were required to allocate ninety-five per cent of their places to such candidates if they presented themselves. So, and only so, I became a prospective university entrant. In the two months or so between demobilisation in July 1946 and my admission to Aberystwyth at the beginning of October 1946, I resumed participation in a local dance band called the 'The Red Aces'. There is no modesty whatsoever in my testimony that the Red Aces fell somewhat short of the Louis Armstrong standard. I had played with this band before the war. The going rate was then ten shillings a night, a night meaning 8 PM until 2 AM, except on Saturday nights when religious sensitivities demanded that the dance ended at midnight. I joined them again in August 1946."[iv]

The REME Sergeant at Work, 1945/46

It was while playing with the Red Aces in the gymnasium of the Llanion Barracks one Saturday night that he first met my mother, then eighteen years of age and visiting her grandmother, who lived in Golden Hill. The rest, as they say, is history. My father later recollected how he had gained her approval by writing an essay for her that she had not started because of the time they had spent together. The essay was due for submission to her Teacher Training College at Matlock the following day.

> *"I came under pressure to write it for her as a kind of moral obligation. The subject was 'Great Expectations', and I consequently found myself writing what I thought was a brilliant essay on a book which in fact I had never read. It received,*

apparently, some considerable commendation, which merely proved that the lecturer concerned never read the book either."[iv]

Their courtship continued with a trip to London which included visits to the Old Bailey, Westminster Abbey and the House of Commons, where

> *"we sought admission – unsuccessfully – to the Public Gallery by trying to get a 'Green Card' from my MP, Major Lloyd George, the Member for Pembroke, but failed to do so as the MP was not in the House. I subsequently learnt that he was very, very seldom in the House."*

It was shortly after this trip that my father proposed, and on December 29th 1947 they were married "in the very modest little church of St Augustine in Wycombe, long since demolished." My father later recalled that,

> *"Even by the standards of those austerity, ration-ridden days, it could hardly be described as a fashion-plate wedding: no great dignitaries, no choir. No professional sopranos, not even the organ to boom out traditional marches. The latter much enraged my elder sister, Doreen, who declared afterwards that, had she known, she would have played the thing herself. The church did not in fact run to an organ but only a somewhat asthmatic harmonium, and Doreen was no great musician, so it was just as well that she found out about the lack of music too late."*[vi]

There followed a modest reception at my mother's home, 221 West Wycombe Road, hosted by her parents.

> *"It was not exactly the social event of the year. At about three in the afternoon we departed in a taxi – my brother, having been Best Man, cadged a lift to the station and travelled up to London with us, departing then to Paddington and leaving us to make our way to an obscure hotel in Queensgate where we spent our three-day honeymoon."*

Wedding Day, December 29th 1947

2 Monetary Policy in War and Peace, 1931–1949

The Mechanism of Cheap Money, 1932-1937

Newly embarked on married life, my father worked hard to make a success of his university career. At undergraduate level, he took a twin degree in Law and Economics at the University College of Wales, Aberystwyth, graduating with a first class honours degree.

At that time in Wales, there were plenty of lawyers but not very many economists. Add to that the fact that my father was intensely curious about the world of money, how it operated, and how fluctuations in its value and availability had caused such hardship to his own family and millions of others during the Great Depression, and his mind was made up. He would continue, as far as he was able, his study of economics.

So, with support of his professors at Aberystwyth, he embarked on postgraduate research into the subject. The title of his thesis was *The Market for Gilt-Edged Securities, 1939–1949*. It was a forensic examination of British monetary policy during the Second World War and its immediate aftermath, supported by copious statistical research and numerous tables supporting a detailed analysis of monetary management during the war years and immediately after. It was never published, so, unless a copy of his 1949 dissertation is buried somewhere in the archives of Aberystwyth University to this day, it may be that the only two extant copies of his dissertation are those that I and my sister Tessa still have in our respective libraries.

His Aberystwyth dissertation was deemed of sufficient quality to gain him the offer of a prized Houblon-Norman Fellowship in 1950. The fellowship was named after the first Governor of the Bank of England, Sir John Houblon, who served between 1694 and 1697, and the longest serving Governor, Montagu Norman, who served between 1920 and 1944. According to the details given about the fellowship on the Bank of England's website, it is "awarded to promote research into, and disseminate knowledge and understanding of, the working, interaction and function of financial institutions in the UK and elsewhere and the economic conditions affecting them," in order to "enable successful applicants to engage in research on an economic or financial topic of their own choice", and was first established in 1944 to celebrate the Bank's 250th anniversary.

My father used the financial support provided by the fellowship to gravitate towards Cambridge, where the ghost of John Maynard Keynes, who had died in 1946, still dominated the economics department. My father's supervisor in the first year of his doctoral research was one of Keynes' closest disciples, Richard Kahn, whose seminal 1931 paper on the multiplier[vii] formed a key element in Keynes' *General Theory of Employment, Interest and Money* when it was published in 1936.

My father did not take to Kahn. I remember him grumbling about how little he saw of his PhD supervisor, and how little feedback he received from him on his evolving research on British monetary policy during the 1930s.

It was only much later, long after my father had passed away, that I came across a possible explanation for Kahn's inattention when I read Sylvia Nasar's *Grand Pursuit: The Story of the People Who Made Modern Economics*[viii]. This elegantly written and thoroughly researched work tells the story of the development of economics through the histories of the women and men who shaped it. The chapter on Joan Robinson, a member of Keynes' inner circle at Cambridge during the 1930s, particularly gripped my attention. In it, Sylvia Nasar tells the story of the on-off affair between Joan Robinson and Keynes' Golden Boy Richard Kahn that began during the early 1930s and endured for many years thereafter.

Here was a possible explanation for Kahn's neglect of his duties as my father's PhD supervisor. Given the choice between an hour spent in the company of a nerdy Welsh postgraduate student, and an hour spent discussing the finer points of Keynesian Theory, or whatever other subjects took their fancy, with Joan Robinson, for some unfathomable reason he seems to have preferred the latter.

Nevertheless, my father played a straight bat in acknowledging Kahn's assistance in the opening paragraphs of *The Mechanism of Cheap Money*.

> *"I was extraordinarily fortunate in having during this time the benefit of guidance in my research from Professor R.F. Kahn during 1950-51 and*

> *Professor Sir Dennis Robertson during 1951-52. The profound impression made by Professor Kahn upon my theoretical approach to the issues discussed in the book will be obvious to anyone familiar with the development of modern monetary thought and with Professor Kahn's outstanding contribution to it."*[ix]

After the first year of his doctoral research he came under the wing of Dennis Robertson, perhaps because the findings emerging from his research were beginning to throw doubt on some of the central tenets of Keynes' *General Theory*, which would hardly have sat comfortably with Richard Kahn. The Acknowledgments on the first page of *The Mechanism of Cheap Money* continue,

> *"To have had the opportunity of continued discussions with, and advice from, Professor Sir Dennis Robertson was inevitably a most stimulating and rewarding experience."*

A third name then appears.

> *"Mr H.G. Johnson, Fellow of King's College, was a constant source of help, in both the technical sphere and otherwise, to a degree which is difficult to adequately acknowledge."*

The friendship forged between Mr Johnson and my father at Cambridge was to endure a lifetime. A near contemporary of my father's, Johnson had already, in his mid-twenties, secured a Fellowship at King's, Keynes' old college, yet was far from being an uncritical follower of

Keynesian Theory or a member of the Cambridge Circus, the inner circle of Keynes' disciples at the university.

Among those who were members of the Circus, my father had little to do with Joan Robinson. Whatever her merits as an economist, she seems to have been a destructive force in her personal relationships. Perhaps, as the only woman in a male-dominated and sometimes misogynist environment, she had to use whatever weapons were at her disposal to get ahead. In her efforts to inveigle her way into Keynes's confidence, she had engineered an irreparable breach between Keynes and Professor Robertson, with whom, whatever their differences on matters of economic theory, Keynes had always previously enjoyed a cordial friendship. A 2009 biography of Joan Robinson[x] observed that,

> *"During the 1920s, the etiquette of Cambridge economists was grounded on a principle of liberal civility: unsparing frankness in debate and an absolute distinction between ideas and persons. Intellectual positions but not their advocates were open to criticism.....(However) in scientific debate and academic disputation, Joan Robinson was not averse to 'ad hominem' tactics that transgressed this etiquette. Moreover, her transgressions exhibited a lack of finesse and tact that suggested malice. As one of Keynes' contemporaries complained to him, "It is a pity she's so bloody rude." (Sir Dennis) Robertson, with whom she clashed on issues of both theory and curriculum, was a favourite object of her invective. Any move*

on Keynes's part that indicated support for the role she was constructing for herself at Cambridge would, it seemed, put him at odds with Robertson."

It is possible that my father was given some quiet advice by Sir Dennis Robertson to stay well clear of Joan Robinson. By contrast, he was most certainly acquainted with her husband Austin, the third member of the unhappy *ménage à trois* of which Joan was centre. My father did not take to him one little bit. Austin Robinson succeeded Keynes as Editor of *The Economic Journal*, and I remember seeing some correspondence between him and my father relating to a paper that my father had submitted for publication in the Journal, which Austin Robinson had opened with the salutation "Dear Nevin." My father would not have appreciated being addressed as if he were some recalcitrant schoolboy. He would have expected to be addressed as "Dear Mr Nevin," or, after he had secured his PhD, "Dear Dr Nevin", or, after gaining a Chair in Economics, as "Dear Professor Nevin." He replied in like fashion, addressing Austin Robinson as "Dear Robinson", but no further submissions followed from him to *The Economic Journal*, obviating the need for any further communication with Austin Robinson.

It was many years later that I last heard my father refer to him. Over lunch one day around the year 1990, he mentioned, with a note of utter contempt in his voice, that Austin Robinson had authorised his wife's life support machine to be switched off. My father simply could not conceive how a man could (as he saw it) approve the death of his own wife.

Whatever titles and distinctions might be bestowed upon Professor Sir Edward Austin Gossage Robinson CMG, OBE, FBA, as far as my father was concerned he would always be a jumped-up supercilious twit; nothing more and nothing less.

[In the interests of balance, I should mention that, at the time of her death, Joan Robinson was reported to have been in a coma for several months[xi]].

****

My father, a rather straitlaced individual, would not have been comfortable with the somewhat louche morality of the Cambridge Circus. He was far happier in the more conventional company of Sir Dennis Robertson. While Robertson lacked Keynes' iconoclastic brilliance and ability to address economic challenges from radically new perspectives, as my father's PhD research progressed he began to suspect that Robertson's classical approach might offer a more accurate insight into the monetary history of the 1930s and 1940s than Keynes' *General Theory*[xii].

One of the central risks highlighted by Keynes in his *General Theory* was that, after a financial crisis such as the Wall Street Crash of 1929 and subsequent bank runs, an economy could fall into a Liquidity Trap. In a Liquidity Trap confidence would be so low that, no matter how far interest rates had fallen and how much credit pumped into the economy, entrepreneurs would be unwilling to borrow to invest in new projects. Keynes likened this trap to "pushing on a string". No matter how hard a string is pushed, it will not move unless someone is pulling it at the other end. Under such circumstances, argued Keynes, monetary policy will be ineffective. The only way out of a slump under such circumstances is a public works programme financed, if need be, by a fiscal deficit – in other words, the government spending more than it is earning in tax revenues.

The Keynesian approach tends to appeal to those on the political left, as this prescription would increase the size and power of the State. The alternative approach, relying on cheap money to stimulate entrepreneurial investment, appeals more to those who favour a greater role for the private sector in the economy and are wary of extensive State control. My father had no particular axe to grind in either direction. What he was interested in was the evidence provided by the 1930s and the worst economic depression in history.

In helping him address this question, he had an unlikely ally in the form of Neville Chamberlain, who served as the Chancellor of the Exchequer in the British Governments of 1931 to 1937, when he became Prime Minister.

Chamberlain today is remembered as a failed Prime Minister who was duped by Adolf Hitler at Munich in 1938, returning to Britain waving a worthless piece of paper declaring that it meant "Peace in our time" and confidently stating that Hitler had promised him that he had "no more territorial demands in Europe" provided that the Sudetenland was ceded to the Reich. This proved to be a complete lie, and, once they had swallowed Czechoslovakia, the Nazis proceeded to invade Poland, precipitating the outbreak of the Second World War in September 1939.

However, although Chamberlain's career as Prime Minister ended in abject failure, years earlier he proved to be a successful Chancellor, and a case could be made for him to be ranked as the most successful British Chancellor of the twentieth century. If Churchill was a terrible Chancellor but a great War Leader, the opposite might be said of Neville Chamberlain.

Chamberlain's first great asset as Chancellor was luck. A few weeks before he went to the Treasury, the Gold Standard collapsed. This had nothing to do with British economic policy; it occurred because of wholly extraneous circumstances. The Wall Street Crash of 1929 led to significant losses for American banks that had advanced funds to speculators who borrowed against the collateral of the shares they owned. When share prices crashed in 1929, many American borrowers were unable to service their debts. American banks then sought to call in their overseas loans to cover their losses, draining gold reserves from other countries. In a desperate attempt to maintain the convertibility of their national currencies into gold, foreign central banks raised their interest rates.

All to no avail. The general increase in interest rates worsened the economic crisis, making it more expensive for individuals and companies to borrow money and leading to higher unemployment. As unemployment rose, pressure on government finances increased because income and corporation tax revenues fell while expenditure on unemployment benefits increased.

In a final effort to sustain the convertibility of Sterling into Gold, the Bank of England more than doubled its Base Rate from 2½ per cent in July 1931 to six per cent in September 1931. The emergency increase in the Base Rate failed to stop outflows of foreign exchange however, and, with its gold reserves running down at an alarming rate, on September 19th 1931 the Bank of England announced that Sterling was no longer convertible into Gold at a fixed rate.

The story goes that, when the final decision was taken for the Pound to come off the Gold Standard, the Governor of the Bank of England, Montagu Norman – one of the Gold Standard's staunchest defenders – was on the high seas, returning to Britain on a transatlantic liner from Canada. His officials at the Bank of England, keen to warn him in advance of the decision to abandon Gold, gave considerable thought to how he could best be informed without divulging this highly market sensitive information to any third party. They finally decided on a six word telegram which ran:

OLD * LADY * GOES * OFF * ON * MONDAY

The Old Lady in question being the Old Lady of Threadneedle Street, the nickname for the Bank of England, while the advice that she "goes off on Monday" was intended as a coded reference to the day when the announcement would be made that Sterling would leave the Gold Standard.

His officials felt confident that the Governor would understand the import of their message. Montagu Norman, after giving careful thought to the telegram, concluded that it was most thoughtful of his deputies to keep him informed about the holiday arrangements of his elderly mother[xiii].

The true meaning of the communication eluded him until he landed back in Britain, by which time Sterling had already plummeted against the US Dollar, falling from £1 = $4.86 to $3.39 by the end of the year.

With the need to defend the Pound now gone, there was no reason for the Bank of England to maintain a high Base Rate, and by the end of June 1932 it had been cut to two per cent. This gave Chamberlain his opportunity. "It was this fall in interest rates which made possible the great War Loan conversion announced at the end of June 1932,"[xiv] reports *The Mechanism of Cheap Money*.

The War Loan comprised money raised by the British Government from patriotic Britons to help finance the war effort during the Great War. It paid a fixed interest rate of five per cent and was repayable at par at any time from June 1929 onwards. According to the estimates given in *The Mechanism of Cheap Money*, at the end of March 1932 no less than £2,085 million of the War Loan – equivalent to approximately £200 billion in 2025 prices – was still outstanding , "representing twenty-seven per cent of the total National Debt and thirty-eight per cent of all British Government securities quoted on the London Stock Exchange."

What Chamberlain proposed was that the Government would repay the five per cent War Loan on December 1st 1932, replacing it with a new 3½ per cent War Loan repayable at par at the Government's option in 1952 or any time thereafter. In other words, the Chancellor was asking holders of the old five per cent War Loan to voluntarily accept a cut of almost a third in their investment income. Holders of the five per cent War Loan could accept cash instead, but this is not what the Treasury wanted – if all holders demanded cash, it would result in an enormous increase in the money supply with unpredictable, but probably highly inflationary, consequences.

It was an audacious gambit on Chamberlain's part with no guarantee of success. But he pulled off "easily the largest conversion operation in the history of the National Debt", as *The Mechanism of Cheap Money* observes.

> *"In the event, no less that £1,921 million, or 92 per cent of the old War Loan, was converted into the new 3½ per cent security, and only £164 million repaid in cash. This was a remarkable result, especially in view of the very scattered holdings of the War Loan."*[xv]

One factor which undoubtedly helped Chamberlain was that prices were falling. The British Retail Price Index fell by almost a fifth between 1922 and 1932, so a 3½ per cent nominal yield on the War Loan prospectively offered a higher real yield if prices continued to fall. Chamberlain and the Treasury sought to persuade their investors this was the best return they were likely to get and the War Loan was the most secure stock on offer, so they would be ill-advised to refuse it. In this, they were assisted by a supportive press. The London *Times*, the house journal of the English middle class, declared on July 25th 1932 that if an investor

> *"should choose to be paid out in cash rather than accept conversion, he will speedily discover that the prices of investments offering any comparable degree of security have so far risen against him that his effort to maintain the return on his capital will be frustrated."*[xvi]

The message was that the British Government's offer was not only fair, but, given the low level of risk in government bonds, better than any other investment likely to be available in the foreseeable future. It may have helped that this message was delivered by a man as uncharismatic as Neville Chamberlain, whose measured delivery reassured even the most nervous investor that their money would be safe in his hands, particularly as he fully intended to achieve at least a budgetary balance in the government's own finances. In fact, by 1934, the Chancellor had achieved a budgetary surplus and was able to reverse previous cuts in unemployment compensation and civil service salaries.

The Mechanism of Cheap Money concluded that

> *"The growth of confidence in the government was a fundamental factor in the fall in interest rates, and that was caused by the belief that the government had firmly adopted the principles of orthodox finance."*

The implication is that Chamberlain's cheap money policy might well not have succeeded had a Keynesian fiscal policy of increased public spending financed by budget deficits been adopted. Chamberlain's success ultimately lay in persuading investors that interest rates were likely to remain low for the indefinite future.

In this, he proved correct. The Base Rate remained at two per cent throughout the 1930s, while the yield on long-term government bonds (Consols) was steady at around three per cent.[xvii] The external value of Sterling was also stable after its initial downward lurch following the abandonment of the Gold Standard. The Bank of England set up an Exchange Equalisation Account to iron out fluctuations in the Pound's external value. If the Pound rose towards an upper limit, the Bank of England would intervene in the foreign exchange market by selling it for gold, dollars and other foreign currencies in order to bring its rate back down again. Conversely, if Sterling threatened to breach a lower limit, the Bank would buy it in order to drive the rate of exchange back up. In this way, the Bank could counter speculative attacks on the Pound and would profit by buying foreign exchange when it was cheap and selling when it was expensive. These tactics would work provided that the UK economy was not running a permanent Balance of Payments deficit. If it was, then demand for foreign currency by overseas exporters to Britain would eventually exhaust the Bank of England's foreign exchange reserves and drive down the Pound.

According to the Keynesian narrative, the recovery of the British economy only began in earnest when it was stimulated by the rearmament programme introduced to counter the growing threat from Nazi Germany from 1936 onwards, some four years after Chamberlain initiated his cheap money policy. Chamberlain's policy was a necessary but not sufficient condition to achieve complete recovery. A well-designed public works programme as advocated by Keynes, funded by government borrowing, could have provided the additional stimulus needed to achieve full employment.

In the event, this stimulus only occurred with the advent of war and the adoption of a fiscal strategy devised by Keynes himself to pay for the war effort.

The War Years, 1939-1945

Historians debate whether Field Marshall Erwin Rommel or Field Marshall Erich von Mannstein were the most effective Second World War Generals for their feats in defeating armies vastly superior to theirs in men and munitions.

Going further back in time, many historians regard Robert E. Lee as the outstanding general of the American Civil War; most historians agree that Napoleon was a military genius; and that Lord George Murray was the most skilful battlefield general of the 1745 Jacobite Rising.

What these generals have in common is that they all ended up on the losing side. Most wars are won, not by the armies with the best generals, but by the nations with the greater resources at their disposal to wage war. Yet, in contrast to the many millions of words published on the military campaigns of the Second World War, comparatively little has been published about the economic strategy that paid for those campaigns. If Britain survived for a year in 1940/41 when, after the fall of France, she stood alone against the might of Nazi Germany, and was then able to go on the offensive after the United States and Russia entered the war in the latter half of 1941, it was in large part due to her success in mobilising the nation's fiscal and monetary resources for the war effort. Indeed, a case could credibly be made that Britain's greatest general of the Second World War was not a soldier at all, but an economist.

Early in the Second World War, in November 1939, John Maynard Keynes set out a strategy for financing the war effort in a series of articles in the London *Times,* subsequently published in the following year in a short book entitled *How to Pay for the War*[xviii]. During the First World War, the British Government operated on the assumption that there was a maximum level of taxation, and a minimum level of spending, that their citizens would accept. If the war effort cost more than the government could raise in taxation, then it would have to borrow the rest and worry about how to repay the debt once the war was over. In *How to Pay for the War,* Keynes challenged the assumption that there was a maximum level of tax that British citizens would be prepared to pay during wartime, and set out proposals to raise additional taxation to fund the war effort.

When Churchill became Prime Minister in May 1940, one of his first Cabinet appointments was that of a trusted lieutenant, Sir Kingsley Wood, as his Chancellor of the Exchequer. Sir Kingsley in turn appointed Keynes as his adviser at the Treasury and the strategy set out in *How to Pay for the War* then formed the basis of his 1941 Budget. The Budget extended the scope of income tax, raised its rate, and increased the amounts levied from purchase tax and import duties. The wartime coalition government also adopted Keynes's proposals to maximise output by mobilising women and previously unemployed workers for wartime work, and recruiting fit workers past normal retirement age and youths who might otherwise have stayed on at school, such as my father, who joined the Ministry of Aircraft Production at the age of sixteen.

Although Keynes's plan resulted in a far higher proportion of war expenditure being funded by taxation than during the First World War, taxes still only covered about half of wartime expenditure. The balance had to be met by borrowing. Early in the war, additional imports were paid for by running down Britain's gold and foreign exchange reserves. However, by the time Churchill became Prime Minister in May 1940, Britain no longer had enough reserves to pay for essential imports. One of his top priorities was therefore to enter into negotiations with the American Government for dollar loans to pay for imports of materiel and supplies needed to sustain the war effort. This culminated in the Lend-Lease Agreement, signed into law by President Franklin D. Roosevelt in March 1941, under which the British Government borrowed a total of $31.4 billion to pay for essential imports.

The British Government also sought to mobilise domestic savings for the war effort. In his postgraduate dissertation, *The Market for Gilt-Edged Securities September 1939-*

December 1949[xix], my father set out in forensic detail the Bank of England's operations in the gilt-edged market during this period. The dissertation provides a blow-by-blow account of the British Government's efforts to raise money during the war.

The government's monetary strategy during this period may be summarised as aiming to raise as much money, as cheaply as possible, for as long as possible. In pursuance of this goal, some £7 billion of new government securities were issued during the war years, equivalent to more than £400 billion in 2024/25 prices, representing three-quarters of the UK's National Income in 1945. Of this amount, approximately £2.7 billion was placed with the 'Big Five' English commercial banks, By the end of the war, no less than two-thirds of bank assets were held in government stock. A further £2 billion of gilts were held by other government departments.

The Government did its best to raise as much money as it could from higher taxes, overseas borrowing and domestic savings. It was not enough. As during the First World War, there was a significant increase in money supply during the war years. On one measure, the UK's money supply increased by £2.9 billion between 1940 and 1945[xx]. There were, inevitably, inflationary consequences, but they were significantly less than in World War One. Whereas the general price level had more than doubled during the First World War, it increased by about a third between 1940 and 1945. British households were sheltered from the worst ravages of inflation by price controls combined with rationing of such essentials as bread, meat and eggs.

Post-War: Dr Dalton and Ultra-Cheap Money, 1945–1949

At the end of the Second World War, approximately £1.2 billion of gilt-edged stock was due for repayment within five years, with an option to repay a further £4 billion within seven years. Add to this the fact that the incoming Labour Government needed additional funds to pay for its ambitious programme of social reform and nationalisation and, even allowing for savings in military spending, it was clear that much of the National Debt would have to be refinanced.

The incoming Chancellor of the Exchequer charged with meeting this formidable challenge was Dr Hugh Dalton. He had a vested interest in maintaining interest rates at as low a level as possible to minimise the government's cost of borrowing. In this, he had an improbable ally in the major commercial banks. If interest rates rose, the value of the government stocks held by the banks would fall and they would suffer significant capital losses. Therefore, the banks too wanted interest rates to remain low in order to give them a breathing space to adjust to post-war conditions.

For a time, Dr Dalton and his Treasury team showed considerable skill in achieving this, placing long-term gilts at 2½ per cent, but it was not to last.

Dalton's ultra-cheap money policy depended on convincing the investing public that interest rates were likely to remain low, so that holding cash in the hope of better returns later was unlikely to prove a profitable strategy. It was the same message that Neville Chamberlain had sold to persuade investors to buy his 3½ per cent War Loan during the early 1930s. However, that was during a time of deflation and economic depression. The circumstances were very different at the end of the Second World War, when wartime restrictions were being eased and pent-up demand released, offering better opportunities for profitable investment than Dalton's 2½ per cent stock. Under the circumstances, the Labour Chancellor perhaps did well to maintain his ultra-cheap money policy for as long as he did. It was not until late in 1946 that it started to unravel.

The turning point came in October 1946, when the government announced that three per cent Local Loans, a stock repayable at par at any time on one month's notice, would be repaid on January 5th 1947. *The Market for Gilt-Edged Securities* reported that,

> *"The only surprising feature of this operation was that it had been so long delayed. With a 2½ per cent level on loans up to twenty years maturity now consolidated in the market, the existence of £429 million of three per cent callable stock could be nothing but an anomaly."*[xxi]

By refinancing the three per cent stock at 2½ per cent, the British Government would save something over £2 million per annum. The ebullient Dr Dalton was delighted at the success of his operation, declaring that it was a landmark in British history – the first time that the government had been able to issue at par, for cash, an irredeemable security yielding just 2½ per cent.

It was a moment of hubris. *The Market for Gilt-Edged Securities* commented drily,

> *"Dr Dalton, in a more than usually buoyant moment, claimed that the hierarchy of London Stock Exchange would one day have a statue built in his memory. While the prospects of this ambition being realised do not at the present time appear particularly bright, the Stock Exchange went some way by dubbing the new Treasury Stock with the name 'Daltons', by which name they are now invariably referred to, although its subsequent career does not perhaps flatter its creator. The majority of investors displayed a marked aversion to the Chancellor's latest form of borrowing, finding little to attract them in a one-way option stock with no guaranteed redemption date and carrying 2½ per cent for at least thirty years."*[xxii]

On the secondary market, the price of the Daltons fell like a stone, leaving any investor subscribing to them nursing significant losses. Among the institutions that had unwisely invested in the Daltons, and lost a great deal of money as a result, was the University College of Wales in Aberystwyth.

Every cloud has a silver lining. It was the failure of the Daltons that led to the suggestion that my father should research the operation of the UK gilt-edged market ten years, as his colleague at Aberystwyth, Professor George Clayton, later recalled.

"His interest in monetary economics began when he was appointed to a Research Studentship and instructed by his head of department to undertake a study of the gilt-edged market. This occurred because the latter had bumped into Nevin – as he told one with a wicked twinkle in his eye – after he had been savaged by the College Investment Committee for recommending the purchase of 2½ per cent Consols at the height of Hugh Dalton's drive for cheap money."[xxiii]

It was not just the domestic bond market that was posing a difficult challenge for Dr Dalton. The British Government also needed to service the UK's obligations under the wartime Lend-Lease Agreement and maintain the convertibility of the £ at $4.03 to pay for essential imports. Temporary respite was provided by a further loan from the American Government negotiated on the British Government's behalf by Maynard Keynes, under which Britain borrowed a further $3.75 billion at two per cent. However, by the time the Anglo-American Loan Agreement was signed on July 15th 1946, Keynes was dead. He passed away at the age of sixty-two, exhausted by this last public service to Britain which followed shortly after he had led British negotiations at Bretton Woods that established the post-war framework for international trade and finance which endured until 1972.

Without Keynes to advise him, Hugh Dalton struggled to sustain his ultra-cheap money policy, as *The Market for Gilt-Edged Securities* recounted.

"Dr Dalton's bull tactics 'par excellence' in the gilt-edged market were beginning to lose their old magic. So long as investors believed that the Chancellor would pursue to the bitter end his policy of ultra-cheap money, whatever the cost, and was therefore ultimately certain to succeed, the Chancellor's work would largely be done for him. Convinced that a 2½ per cent basis would be secured in long-term market, and that capital values would rise accordingly, full-scale buying would ensue until 2½ per cent was in fact established. Once let that confidence in the Chancellor's power and determination falter, however, and the reverse process is inevitable. What was occurring at the beginning 1947 was growing doubts among investors as to the Government's willingness to permit an inflationary policy to be conducted for the sake of lower rates of interest at a time when there was growing awareness of the menace of inflation at home and its related dangers in the sphere of the overseas trading account. That this confidence was faltering is reflected, not so much in the general gilt-edged index, as in the prices of irredeemable securities, always the most sensitive indicators of market sentiment."[xxiv]

Meanwhile, the conditions attached to the July 1946 Anglo-American Loan Agreement were beginning to bite, in particular the commitment to make Sterling convertible in July 1947, one year after the loan was ratified. Within a month of this trigger date, nations with Sterling balances in London had withdrawn almost a billion dollars from British reserves, forcing the British Government to suspend the convertibility of the Pound and implement drastic cuts in public expenditure.

Hugh Dalton did not long survive as Chancellor of the Exchequer after the Sterling Crisis of the summer of 1947. In November, he inadvertently let slip some details of his forthcoming Budget to a reporter minutes before delivering his budget speech. When the news was printed in the early editions of evening newspapers while he was still on his feet in the House of Commons and the Stock Market still open, he tendered his resignation, which the Prime Minister, Clement Attlee, accepted with some alacrity.

By late 1949, yields on the Daltons had increased from 2½ per cent to just over 3½ per cent. The increase in interest rates did not attract enough foreign exchange into London, and on September 18th 1949 Sterling was devalued by almost a third from $4.03 to $2.80.

Reflecting on post-war monetary policy, *The Market for Gilt-Edged Securities* concluded that,

> *"Demand for investment finance in excess of the supply of savings will place downward pressure on the prices of gilt-edged securities. The lesson of the Daltonian campaign was that this pressure may for a time be reversed by credit injection on a sufficiently wide scale, but if investors fear that credit injections will result in an upsurge of inflation*

then the only way in which a cheap money policy can be maintained is through the achievement of a sufficiently large budgetary surplus to bring total savings into equality with total investment.[xxv]

Concluding Comments

Three guiding principles emerge from the analysis of British monetary policy provided by *The Mechanism of Cheap Money* and *The Market for Gilt-Edged Securities*, of which any government would be prudent to take note.

The first is that the combination of cheap money and a loose fiscal policy is likely to prove inflationary and socially disruptive. This principle is borne out by British experience during the 1970s and early 2020s.

The second is that a cheap money policy, under which the Central Bank seeks to minimise the cost of its borrowing by maintaining low interest rates on both its short-term loans (Treasury Bills) and its longer term debt, can be sustained if fiscal policies are tight. Provided that the government raises tax revenues sufficient to cover public expenditure, and runs a primary budget surplus, investors are likely to commit their funds to new debt issues at or below existing yields.

The third general principle is that a loose fiscal policy, under which government expenditure is not fully funded by taxation revenues, is likely to prove increasingly expensive, because investors will require ever higher yields to invest in government bonds. The bond market itself may therefore place a constraint on the government's ability to pursue a loose fiscal policy, as the short-lived government of Liz Truss discovered to its cost during the Fall of 2022.

Bond investors may accept a loose fiscal policy for a limited period if it has a clear rationale, such as national defence, a major emergency such as the Covid pandemic, or the need to drive recovery from a deep recession. However, the government must have a credible strategy for returning to budgetary balance over the medium term. If not, investors may fear that budget deficits will lead to rising levels of public debt, and the cost of servicing this debt will rise, resulting in losses for anyone holding it.

The Market for Gilt-Edged Securities was not intended to predict the future, but rather to analyse the recent past. However, it did conclude with some tentative forecasts for the 1950s in the light of the position prevailing in September 1950 when it was submitted. Its main prediction was that both inflation and the yields on long-term government stock (Consols) were likely to be higher during the 1950s than they had been during the 1930s. Both forecasts proved correct. The annual rate of increase in the UK retail price index averaged four per cent during the 1950s compared to zero per cent during the period between 1930 and 1939.[xxvi] Similarly, while the yield on Consols had averaged 3½ per cent during the 1930s and three per cent during the war and immediate post-war periods, it rose to 4½ per cent during the 1950s, and by 1960 was above five per cent and rising. This in turn placed a heavier burden on the British Government in servicing the National Debt. This was the problem addressed in my father's first book, published by the University of Wales Press in 1954.

3 The Problem of the National Debt

The funding that my father had secured in 1950 from the Houblon-Norman Fellowship was for two years. As that source of funds neared an end and his PhD research neared completion, he began to look around for a job. Of the many applications submitted, two came up trumps – one in Madison, Wisconsin, a move vetoed by my mother, and another in Australia, which my father decided against, for reasons explained in his 1983 memoir.

> *"Australia sounded attractive enough except for a thoroughly pessimistic picture painted for me about the prospects of finding reasonable housing on arrival: standard practice was apparently for immigrants to spend a considerable time in government camps built for the purpose. That was pretty well conclusive. Two continents had now been robbed of our citizenship within the single month of March 1952."*[xxvii]

Towards the end of March, my father responded to two further job advertisements – one a junior lecturing post at Aberystwyth, the other at the Organisation for European Economic Co-operation (OEEC) in Paris. A job offer came through quite quickly from Aberystwyth, so in July 1952 he went back to Cambridge for the last time to "change the last cheque from the Bank of England and see Professor Robertson", taking my older brother Paul with him. His 1983 Memoir records that,

"I parked Paul on a window ledge outside Robertson's rooms in Trinity while I went in to take my leave. Spotting this young infant, Robertson, a lifelong bachelor, took great pains to show Paul around a collection he had of carved animals, a present to him from Lidya Lopokova, the ballet dancer, more celebrated in Cambridge as the widow of Maynard Keynes. Paul was more impressed with a small trap-door in the main door of Robertson's set of rooms which the great man explained had been put there for his cat to enter and leave."[xxviii]

By September, and the beginning of the new academic year, the family were back in Aberystwyth as my father embarked on an academic career. Reflecting on his time in Cambridge, he wrote that,

"From a strictly personal point of view we had been happy enough in Cambridge: we had already reached the point at which we had become, in a sense, strictly self-sufficient, with our own home and growing family to constitute a small universe of our own which we were to occupy for many, many years to follow. But in a more conventional sense Cambridge had not been a great success: we had missed the sea and the hills and disliked the harsh climate; the people had seemed to us cold and distant; and Cambridge then had been a place of two separate worlds in which we had inhabited the outer, unprivileged half. Returning to the less

pretentious, relaxed world of Aberystwyth was in a sense returning to our own world."[xxix]

One Cambridge colleague with whom my father did remain close was the youthful Fellow of King's College, Mr H. G. Johnson. Like my father, Johnson was something of an outsider in the Cambridge of the early 1950s, where the Economics Department was still very much under the shadow of the late, great John Maynard Keynes. Neither my father nor Mr Johnson were members of the Keynesian Cambridge Circle, nor were they fully signed up to the Keynesian Revolution in economic theory, focused as it was on fiscal policy to the neglect of monetary economics. In a generous salute to Mr Johnson, my father closed the Foreword to his first book, *The Problem of the National Debt*, as follows:

> *"I cannot forbear from mentioning my generous and distinguished friend, Mr H.G. Johnson, Fellow of King's College Cambridge. This entire study, in fact, originated in an idea thrown out by him while he was walking and I was struggling along the road which leads up from the sea at Clarach. Since that day, I suspect that he has become separated from my development of the idea in more than a merely geographic sense. In any case I am solely responsible for the views expressed in these pages. The truth of the matter, I suppose, is that he should be credited with more or less anything of merit which this book may by chance contain; the rest is all mine."*[xxx]

Two men on a Welsh Beach, possibly discussing the National Debt?

Gareth C. Thomas 1955-2019, "The Sea and the Hills" (Author's Collection)

So who was Mr H.G. Johnson?

Harry Gordon Johnson was a Canadian economist just twenty months older than my father. Discovering that they shared a common interest in monetary economics and the hospitality of Cambridge taverns during the early 1950s, they forged an intellectual alliance that was to endure a lifetime. Harry Johnson left Cambridge after being appointed Professor of Economics at Manchester University at the age of thirty-three in 1956. From Manchester, he moved on to the University of Chicago where he was appointed Professor in 1959. He was simultaneously Professor of Economics at the London School of Economics from 1966 until 1974, bestriding the world of economics like a Colossus, with one foot in the

Keynesian camp of the LSE and the other in the Monetarist school of Chicago University.

I remember meeting him when he visited us in Swansea during the early Seventies together with his wife Elizabeth, herself an economist of some repute who was one of the Editors of Keynes' Collected Papers. While Harry Johnson was a big man who reminded me of Orson Welles, his wife Elizabeth was a petite blonde who got on well with my mother. I liked Harry Johnson, who was easy to talk to and showed a genuine interest in the life and views of a sixteen year old youth, as I then was, his conversation generously lubricated with supplies from my father's drinks cabinet which, sadly, I was not invited to share. The story goes that, during his weekly flight between London and Chicago to fulfil lecturing duties in each city, he would board each flight with a bottle of Southern Comfort and leave it with a fully written paper ready for publication. I sought to apply the Johnson method myself on one long-haul flight. It is my sad duty to report that, while I completed the first part successfully by consuming a large amount of alcohol, no original insights into the workings of the modern economy emerged as a result.

However, even Harry Johnson could not sustain this lifestyle indefinitely. He suffered a stroke not long after his visit to Swansea and died at the age of fifty-three in 1977. My father later recalled that, as the two of them were walking across Singleton Park outside Swansea's University College late one afternoon, Harry gazed across Swansea Bay and up to the Mumbles, bathed in the setting sun. "You know, Ted, I may be at the cutting edge of thinking on monetary theory at the LSE and Chicago, while here you are, teaching at what some might regard as a provincial backwater", he said, somewhat wistfully, "but I think you may have the better part of the deal."

"The Better Part of the Deal". A Gower Beach in Wintertime.

Gareth C. Thomas 1955-2019, "Winter Sun, Three Cliffs Bay" (Author's Collection)

During his relatively short career, Harry Johnson published over five hundred professional articles, forty books and pamphlets, and one hundred and fifty book reviews. According to Nobel Laureate Paul Samuelson, Harry Johnson had eighteen papers ready for publication when he died. Samuelson commented with some justice "That is dying with your boots on!" Another Nobel Laureate, James Tobin, called the third quarter of the twentieth century between 1950 and 1975 'The Age of Johnson' because of his seminal contributions to monetary and international trade theory, including the part he played in bringing the two together in his monetary approach to the Balance of Payments.

All this lay in the future when the conversation with Harry Johnson inspired my father to write his first book back in 1954.

My father dedicated it to his parents, "acknowledging a much greater debt." Long since out of print, it addressed a problem that was apparently solved by the 1960s and did so in dense, arcane language supported by copious statistical tables which do not make for easy reading. It might therefore be easy to conclude that *The Problem of the National Debt* merits little attention today.

However, upon closer examination, a comparison of Britain's National Debt in the mid-2020s today with the position prevailing some seventy years ago is instructive.

****

The Problem of the National Debt is a monograph approximately one hundred pages in length, whose aim, as set out in its opening words, "is primarily to provoke reflection and discussion on the role of national debt in our economic system, a question which, as far as I know, has never been treated in full in any published work in this country."

At the time of its publication, the UK's National Debt was twice its National Income, and the Debt-to-GDP ratio was "more than twenty times as large in 1950 as it was a mere third of a century earlier." The concern was that the cost of servicing this level of debt would place a heavy burden on the taxpayer and constrain public expenditure for the foreseeable future.

On the face of it, the challenge of managing the National Debt was much greater in the mid-1950s when the book was written than in the mid-2020s. Today, the Debt-to-GDP ratio is half what it was seventy years ago. The contemporary Treasury and the Bank of England may also find comfort in the fact that, during the 1950s and 1960s, Britain's National Debt fell from twice the level of her National Income to just half in 1970 and a quarter in 1990. It is true that the Debt-to-GDP rose rapidly in the first quarter of the 21st century; however, the Treasury and Bank may console themselves that this is due to one-off factors, notably the government's bailout of the banking sector during the global financial crisis of 2007–2009 and the Covid pandemic of 2020–2022. These crises now having passed, one would expect the Debt-to-GDP ratio to progressively fall over time, as it did half a century ago.

However, closer analysis suggests that such a conclusion may be overly sanguine. By 2020, the Debt-to-GDP ratio had risen to the highest level ever recorded during a normal peacetime period not preceded by a major war. There is therefore no possibility of a "demobilisation bonus" such as occurred after the end of these wars, as members of the armed forces returned to civilian employment, factories manufacturing munitions converted to consumer goods, and the burden of military expenditure was slashed. During post-war periods these factors led to a significant improvement in the government's fiscal position, generating additional resources that enabled the Exchequer to pay off maturing debt. They also provided a shot in the arm to economic growth. The real rate of growth of the British economy averaged 3½ per cent a year during the Fifties and Sixties, and even in the more sluggish Seventies and Eighties growth was almost 2½ per cent a year. By contrast, since 1990, the growth rate has fallen to barely one per cent a year. The result is that taxation revenues rose far more slowly in the first quarter of the 21st century than during the last half of the 20th, severely restricting the British Government's ability to pay off its debt.

Moreover, the cost of servicing the debt was lower in the 1950s than seventy years later. Despite the failure of Hugh Dalton's ultra-cheap money campaign of the late 1940s, the average yield on undated government stock (Consols) was approximately 3¾ per cent in 1954 compared to 4½ per cent in 2024, while the Bank of England's Base Rate was three per cent in late 1954 compared to 5¼ per cent in 2024.

The Problem of the National Debt calculated that,

> *"While the apparent burden of National Debt interest payments during 1953 was slightly below five per cent of National Income, the net burden, after allowing for payments to public departments and the banking system and for income taxation payments on interest earned by private investors was less than two per cent."*[xxxi]

What has made the cost of servicing the National Debt even greater at the time of writing, in 2024, is a new class of government stock introduced since the 1950s, index-linked gilts. The repayment cost of this stock rises in line with the UK Retail Price Index (RPI). Data provided by the Bank of England's Debt Management Office revealed that the amount that the British Government received from index-linked gilts when first issued was £377 billion. However, because their repayment is linked to inflation, the Government was due to repay £610 billion as at May 2024[xxxii]. In other words, the Government was obliged to repay £1.62 for every £1 of index-linked stock it had issued, and this amount would only rise over time along with the Retail Prices Index, making index-linked stock easily the most expensive form of government borrowing.

Quite what Harry Johnson and my father would have made of index-linked gilts is unknown, but one suspects that it would not have met with their unqualified approval. Harry Johnson was one of the pioneers of the Monetary Approach to the Balance of Payments, which posits that inflation can be generated by international monetary growth as well as domestic credit expansion. The final cost to the British Government of index-linked stock – which in 2024 represented a quarter of all public debt – is therefore beyond the control of the Treasury or the Bank of England. To have issued debt under such conditions could be deemed reckless.

Higher borrowing costs and the rising burden of index-linked gilts implied that the cost of servicing the National Debt was higher as a percentage of the UK's National Income in 2024 than in 1954. The Office for Budget Responsibility reported in March 2024 that

> *"in 2024-25 we expect debt interest spending to total £89 billion. That would represent 7.3 per cent*

of total public spending and is equivalent to nearly 3.2 per cent national income."[xxxiii]

In short, the lack of any demobilisation bonus, combined with a much slower rate of economic growth and higher cost of borrowing in the mid-2020s compared to the mid-1950s, all point to the worrying conclusion that the problem of the National Debt may prove more intractable today than seventy years ago.

Yet today the Treasury seems largely unconcerned about the scale and structure of the National Debt. Its focus is on cutting taxes or increasing public expenditure, the precise balance depending on the politics of the Chancellor of the Exchequer. Yet the spiralling cost of the National Debt may in the end stymie both aspirations.

****

So what can be done to address this challenge?

The Problem of the National Debt concluded with radical proposals to restructure the debt according to who holds it, reducing its total cost to the taxpayer by adapting its terms to the specific requirements of four distinct categories of investor.

The first category comprises government departments and other public sector bodies. Interest payments to them do not represent a net cost to the government because the cost of interest paid by the Treasury is exactly balanced by income from interest receipts accruing to other public agencies. The net impact of these charges on public sector finances is therefore zero. *The Problem of the National Debt* proposed that public sector agencies should be required to hold all their reserves in a separate category of gilt-edged stock of which they would be the only holders. These gilts would be paid a low rate of interest, which perhaps today would equate to the Bank of England's inflation target, so that the reserves of public sector bodies would maintain their real value over time, but no more.

The second category identified in *The Problem of the National Debt* is commercial banks and other regulated financial institutions, which are required by law to hold some of their reserves at the Bank of England. *The Problem of the National Debt* proposed that these institutions be issued with Government Debt Certificates which would progressively replace their gilt holdings as they matured, bearing a lower rate of interest than conventional gilts. The *quid pro quo* of these arrangements would be enhanced banking stability, as "the commercial banks would be freed from the dangers of market fluctuations in capital values." The lower rate of interest payable on this portion of government debt could be regarded as an insurance premium to cover the costs that the taxpayer bears in order to underwrite the stability of the British banking system, which can be considerable, as evidenced by the global financial crisis of 2008–2009.

The third category is other institutional holders of gilt-edged stock such as major pension and insurance funds, which, like regulated commercial banks, seek predictable cash flows and stable capital values in order to meet their obligations as they fall due. *The Problem of the National Debt* proposed that this class of investor might be issued with a separate class of government stock, offering a higher rate of interest than paid to commercial banks, but a lower rate than on the open market, in return for partial underwriting by the Bank of England, perhaps through repurchase options at a guaranteed minimum value exercisable at any time though to maturity.

The final category comprises all other private investors, including investment trusts, venture capital funds, and private investors wishing to hold part of their reserves in government stock. This fourth category would operate on the open market, with the price of government bonds determined by supply and demand, exposing these investors to potential loss if interest rates rise, but also offering the prospect of capital gains if interest rates fall.

The Problem of the National Debt concluded that,

> *"By converting the debt into this form, the authorities would be able to design it in a way more likely to serve the purposes of the national debt in the modern economy. The aim would be to insulate, as far as is desirable and possible, the three broad groups of debt held outside the government itself, fixing the terms of borrowing for each group independently and in accordance with the special requirements of the group concerned."*[xxxiv]

Seventy years on, the ideas stimulated by a conversation between my father and Harry Johnson on a beach in West Wales all those years ago merit reappraisal. For the dragon of the National Debt is not slain, but merely sleeping.

4 Capital Funds in Emerging Economies

Around the time that my father was writing *The Problem of the National Debt*, a hiatus occurred in his professional and family life that had almost catastrophic results. This was before I was born, so the record I have of the events that followed comes from his unpublished 1983 family memoir.

At the end of his time in Cambridge, when he had been looking for jobs, he had applied for a post with the Organisation for European Economic Corporation (OEEC) in Paris. Hearing nothing from the OEEC, he had accepted the offer of a lectureship in Aberystwyth on a salary of £550 per annum, equivalent to approximately £20,000 in 2024/25 prices. A modest enough stipend, but, as my father wrote,

> *"while money was none too plentiful, we had a place of our own, Aberystwyth was a pleasant little town and I had my feet on the academic ladder – the bottom rung, to be sure, but firmly enough. It was a good department, with an unusually good head, Arthur Beacham, whom we liked and we had quite a few friends (including) Harry and Liz Johnson, who came to stay from Cambridge in March 1953."*[xxxv]

Harry Johnson's visit in March 1953 was the occasion of their walk together at Clarach which inspired *The Problem of the National Debt*.

A few months later, on July 13th 1953, an official letter arrived offering him a job at the OEEC, which was, he wrote, "then unquestionably the powerhouse of applied economics in post-war Europe, which would do me no professional harm." It also offered a salary of £2,500 a year, or approximately £90,000 in today's money, almost five times his academic salary. He still owed £500 to his mother-in-law, who had generously lent her daughter and son-in-law these funds to enable them to buy a modest house in Gwydir Street in Cambridge which they had subsequently sold at a small loss. The OEEC salary would enable them to repay that loan and would have "opened up undreamed-of possibilities like a tax-free car and a severance payment (after two years) which to my eyes looked like the riches of Croesus."

He decided to take the job. For reasons that are not fully explained – perhaps she was concerned that a move to Paris would disrupt the early education of Paul, Tessa and Mary – my mother decided that she could not live in Paris and opted to stay in Aberystwyth.

> *"Elizabeth and I agreed that our only tactic was to save as much as possible from my princely salary to minimise the time I was to spend in Paris – she lived on one quarter of my salary and I lived on another quarter."* [xxxvi]

However, it was not to prove a happy time for either of them.

> *"It was an undeniably lonely existence. The work was interesting enough, but to return night after*

night to a rather chilly attic in the middle of Versailles fell somewhat short of the customary image of the bachelor let loose in Gay Paree. I missed her more and more every day – indeed I even found, to my astonishment, that I missed the three noisy and smelly infants I had left in her charge. After a month following my return after Christmas 1953 I had had enough and gave notice to the OEEC that I was quitting at the end of June. This was greeted in the organisation with some displeasure and considerable surprise: to qualify for the very handsome gratuities provided for in the organisation a minimum of two years' service was required, and after only one I would get nothing. Even more to the point, at that stage, with a wife and three children to support, I had no future job of any kind go to. But, belatedly, I had seen the obvious: money can have too high a price and I was certainly paying it."[xxxvii]

Meanwhile, "back in Aberystwyth, January and February were pretty awful months that year: when it wasn't raining it was snowing; all the children seem to have been unwell sometime or other." Worse was to follow. In April of 1954 my mother was diagnosed with tuberculosis.

"In this day and age, tuberculosis is almost unknown, and when it does occur a moderate dosage of modern antibiotics will see it off in no time at all. In the 1930s and 1940s, however, it was endemic and almost always terminal. Even in the 1950s it carried an aura of fear." [xxxviii]

On April 7th 1954, my father returned home to Aberystwyth. On April 26th, another X-ray brought better results: my mother recorded in her diary that, "the doctor called to say I've no tuberculosis and can get up again gradually." Leaving their three children with their grandparents, my father and mother travelled back to France, where they lived in a small town between Paris and Versailles called St Cloud while my father served his notice with the OEEC. In the summer of 1954 they returned to Aberystwyth, where, thanks to the good offices of Professor Beacham, my father was able to take up his lectureship at the University once more. I was born the following May and Christine followed eighteen months later in November 1956. We can thus fairly claim to be the unplanned progeny of perhaps the world's most financially irrational economist.

****

The year 1957 marked the apogee of my grandfather's political career when he became Mayor of the Royal and Ancient Borough of Pembroke. First elected in 1945 as Councillor for the Pater Ward in Pembroke Dock under the Co-operative Party banner – the Party then being a constituent member of the larger Labour Party – his great mission in the ensuing years had been to rebuild a community centre for the town to replace the old Temperance Hall blitzed during the war. Now, as Mayor, he was to finally achieve his ambition.

A photograph of the day of his inauguration as Mayor of Pembroke on May 22nd 1957 shows, from left to right as we look at it, my brother Paul, my grandmother (the new

Lady Mayoress), my sister Mary, my grandfather in his mayoral robes, my father and my sister Tessa. I and my younger sister Christine – who was a baby of just six months' old at the time – were too young to attend, so were being looked after by my mother back in Aberystwyth

The Inauguration of a new Mayor, May 22nd 1957.

One point that emerges from local news coverage of the event is the much higher degree of courtesy and respect in public discourse compared to today. For example, the outgoing Mayor, Alderman Gwilliam, whom I suspect was not of the same political persuasion as my grandfather, was quite fulsome in the toast he gave to his successor at the modest mayoral lunch held on the day, declaring, according to a contemporary local newspaper report, that

> *"I've always found the Mayor to be a very loyal colleague, and loyalty in public life is an invaluable*

asset. Alderman Nevin enters fully into team spirit and is always prepared to cooperate wholeheartedly in all efforts to promote the betterment of Pembroke and Pembroke Dock. Mean and petty intrigues are completely foreign to his nature."[xxxix]

Echoing these sentiments, the senior Alderman for the Pater Ward, Alderman W.G. Munro, is quoted in the same article as saying,

> *"Alderman Nevin is a son of the Borough and has spent the whole of his lifetime here except the period during the First World War, when he fought in defence of his country in the Balkans and in France. All his children followed the example of their father by doing some form of national service during the 1939-45 war."*

Referring to his work on the Council, Alderman Munro said that, under his chairmanship of the Pater Ward lighting committee, Pembroke Dock had become one of the best lit towns in the country. The results of these endeavours can still be seen today in the street lamps on Dimond Street, evocative of the *Art Noveau* style of my grandfather's youth at the turn of the nineteenth and twentieth centuries.

Whatever their nominal political persuasions, whether Conservative, Liberal or Labour, the men and women on Pembroke Council, and their respective families, had all gone through World Wars, and many of them had served in the armed forces during those wars. This common experience helped to seal a mutual respect and a common desire, once a decision had been arrived at, to pull together for the betterment of the (reasonably prosperous) county town of Pembroke and its (rather poorer) neighbour, the garrison town of Pembroke Dock. They worked together under the Mayor's leadership to build the new Pater Hall on Dimond Street, which opened its doors for the first time in December 1957 as the community hub of Pembroke Dock. A photo of the official opening shows my grandmother unveiling a plaque at the entrance to the Pater Hall, which to this day is run as a charity staffed by dedicated volunteers.

The Official Opening of the Pater Hall, Pembroke Dock, December 11th 1957.

The plaque reads as follows:

"This building, originally constructed in the year 1868 by William Griffiths of this town, at his own expense, for the use of the Total Abstinence Society, was destroyed by enemy action on 2nd September 1940....The Trustees of the society dedicated the damaged premises to the Pembroke Borough Council who rebuilt it in its present form...The new building was opened by His Worship the Mayor (Alderman W. Nevin) on Wednesday 11th December 1957. This commemorative plaque was unveiled by the Mayoress (Mrs W. Nevin)."

My father was not present at the official opening of Pater Hall, for reasons given in a news report in a local Pembroke newspaper:[xl]

"Sailed for Jamaica. Dr Edward Nevin, son of the Mayor and Mayoress, sailed from Liverpool on Tuesday to take up his new appointment as Head of the External Finance Division of Jamaica's Ministry of Finance. Dr Nevin, who was accompanied by his wife and children, has been seconded from his post as Lecturer in Economics at the University College of Wales, Aberystwyth. They are voyaging on the luxury liner 'Reina del Pacifico', which called in at Milford Haven some time ago for repairs shortly after she had made world headlines by running onto a coral reef during a world cruise."

So with this piece of reassuring intelligence to encourage us, we set sail for the West Indies.

Many years afterwards, my late brother-in-law Harry Smith regaled the patrons of the Newton Inn in Mumbles with a story of how "Harold Macmillan had personally hand-picked Ted to help the Jamaican Government prepare for independence."

It was only some time later, when the effect of the Newton Inn's amber nectar had fully worn off, that it occurred to me that it seemed rather unlikely that Mr Macmillan, the Prime Minister of the day, wrestling as he was with challenges like the Winds of Change sweeping through Africa, the Profumo Affair, or indeed the existential threat to humanity posed by the Cuban Missile Crisis, would have spent a great deal of his time pacing Downing Street pondering the appointment of a young university lecturer to a job in the Finance Ministry of a remote Caribbean island.

The truth of how my father came to be offered the post was more prosaic, if equally curious, as recorded in his 1983 memoir.

> *"On July 12th 1957, a letter arrived completely out of the blue from a man called Richardson, who was then the Financial Secretary of the Government of Jamaica, a post roughly corresponding to that of Permanent Secretary to the Treasury in Britain. I had never met, nor even heard of, this gentleman, but the latter announced that he had sought the advice of his old tutors in Oxford (he had been a Rhodes Scholar there) who were Professor J.R. Hicks and his wife Ursula – later Sir John and Lady Hicks, the former being a Nobel Prizewinner. As a result, he was inviting me to take an appointment for two years in Jamaica to assist in the creation of a*

Central Bank as befitted the forthcoming independent status of the island. I was enraptured by the prospect of not merely seeing the far-off world of the Caribbean, but in doing so have a hand in actually creating a new central bank – something which, to put it mildly, relatively few academics have done." [xli]

Unlike the earlier OEEC appointment, on this occasion, happily, my mother agreed that the family should travel together to make a new home in Jamaica. My father's Head of Department in Aberystwyth, Professor Beacham, used his good offices to persuade the college authorities to give him leave of absence to take up the position. However, he was only able to do so after overcoming the obstacle of the Colonial Office. His memoir records that,

"I was not to learn until much later that this initiative of Richardson's had been fiercely resisted by the Colonial Office, which was at that time rightly regarded as the most reactionary department of the British Government with the possible exception of the Home Office. As a result, there followed a succession of arrangements and cancellations of our travelling plans communicated by a series of telegrams from London – including one stormy interview I had with the Colonial Office in London which ended with my abruptly leaving with a declaration that I proposed to report the preceding discussion to my old friend (!) the late Colonial Secretary, Mr James Griffiths. (Indeed, only after we had been on the island more than a year

did I discover that I had been declared persona non grata at the Governor's Residence, a fact which caused us no distress whatever). Losing patience with London, on September 11th I got in the car and drove to Liverpool to enquire personally with the shipping line, the Pacific Steam Navigation Company, which operated the only regular passenger service to the West Indies. If the Colonial Office were incapable of finding accommodation for us all, I thought I would see what I could do on my own behalf." [xlii]

Quite how much influence my father had with the veteran Labour MP and erstwhile Secretary of State for the Colonies, Jim Griffiths MP, is unclear. One suspects that they were, at best, nodding acquaintances. But the threat of bringing down the wrath of the Welsh lobby and perhaps even the entire Labour Party – Griffiths at that time being Deputy Leader of the Opposition – onto the Colonial Office seems to have done the trick. Six days after my father's trip to Liverpool, on September 17th 1957, we embarked for Jamaica, arriving at Kingston two and a half weeks later on October 4th.

****

The relationship between a Minister and his or her senior officials is a complex one, and, if it is to work well, both parties must respect their different roles and responsibilities.

The Minister's role is to set out the government's policy clearly and succinctly. The principal objective of my father's ministerial boss in Jamaica, the Hon Noel Nethersole, was to mobilise the savings of Jamaica's citizens for their benefit, rather than the benefit of her colonial masters.

Once policy is defined, the role of officials is to advise the Minister on possible options for its achievement and undertake work to assess the costs and benefits of different options. On the basis of this assessment, officials may be asked by the Minister to submit recommendations as to which option to pursue.

The Minister may probe his officials' recommendations, testing them to confirm that they have taken into account all relevant factors before arriving at a final decision. The Minister's decision may not follow an official recommendation. Whereas a civil service recommendation is likely to be largely based on technical analysis, a ministerial decision may take account of wider political considerations and voter concerns of which an official may not be fully aware. Provided the Minister and his senior officials work in an atmosphere of mutual courtesy, officials should be able to respect a ministerial decision even when it does not follow their recommendations.

The evidence suggests that this was very much the relationship my father enjoyed with Jamaica's Finance Minister, so much so that he dedicated a book that was inspired by this phase of his career, *Capital Funds in Underdeveloped Countries*, to Mr Nethersole. When one remembers that his only other dedications were to members of his immediate family – *The Problem of the National Debt* to his parents, and *The Mechanism of Cheap*

Money to his wife (my mother) – it can be appreciated in what esteem he held his ministerial boss.

The Head of External Finance, Jamaica 1958.

My father in his office in Kingston, Jamaica, in July 1958.

In a photograph taken of my father in his office at the Ministry of Finance in July 1958, it will be noted that there is no mobile phone – the mobile hadn't been invented then; nor is there a laptop, because laptops had not been invented either; and above all, there is no Internet, whose invention lay more than a quarter of a century in the future. It mattered little. What mattered more were successful working relationships with his political boss, the Minister of Finance, the Hon Noel Nethersole, and the departmental head, the Financial Secretary, the Hon E.R. Richardson.

****

Noel Newton Nethersole was born on November 2nd 1903 in Kingston, Jamaica, the eighth of ten children. He was educated at Jamaica College where he was an outstanding student, and was nominated as the island's Rhodes Scholar for 1923, studying law at Lincoln College, Oxford. He returned to Jamaica in 1926 to practise law, and also played first-class cricket for Jamaica, making his debut in 1926–27. He later served as a member of the West Indies Cricket Board of Control from 1939 to 1955. As a West Indian selector his influence was critical in securing the appointment of George Headley as the first non-white captain of the West Indies cricket team for the series against England in 1947–1948, believing, in the later words of Martin Luther King, that a man should be judged, not by the colour of his skin, but by the content of his character.

Nethersole helped found the Jamaican People's National Party (PNP) in 1938 and served as its vice-president from 1938 onwards under Norman Manley as the Party's president. He was elected to the Jamaican Parliament in 1949, and when the PNP won office in 1955 was appointed Minister of Finance. His mission in office was to modernise Jamaica's financial institutions and achieve economic, as well as political, independence for the island.

One of the major achievements of his period in office was the flotation of the Government of Jamaica's first sovereign bond, which raised $12.5 million, equivalent to approximately $150 million in 2025 prices, on the New York Stock Exchange. Though hardly noted in the history books of the era, it marked a key moment in Jamaica's evolution from a British colony to a fully independent nation state. For the first time, the Jamaican Government did not have to rely on the allocation of funds from London in order to finance its investment programme, but was able to raise funds in its own right as a sovereign borrower.

The negotiation of the loan was not without its pitfalls, as my father recalled in his memoir. It recorded that he and my mother were invited to out dinner by one of the American bond underwriters, a certain Jacob Emerson Thors, on December 11th 1958.

> *"We dined at the Jamaica Inn and then proceeded to the Glass Bucket for post-prandial drinks as his guest. To my infinite dismay, when we subsequently received a statement of fees and expenses from our underwriting friends in New York, the Government of Jamaica was requested to pay the (quite formidable) bill for this gracious hospitality. In the Glass Bucket our host was so enthusiastic about a number the band had struck up – 'Volare' it was called – that he insisted that Elizabeth dance with him, which she did with considerably more sense of duty than enthusiasm. I can never hear 'Volare' without seeing the bald pate and luxuriant moustache of Mr Jacob Emerson Thors."*[xliii]

Happily, despite this experience, the bond issue was concluded a couple of months later, on February 5th 1959.

The occasion is one of my earliest memories because my father bought a toy Tonka dump truck as a present for me at the airport in New York on his way home. Sadly long since lost to posterity, for many years the toy dump truck was my pride and joy.

There is in our family album a photograph of the Jamaican Government team who went to New York to close the deal, taken on their return from New York to Montego Bay at 1:00 a.m. on February 6th 1959. Even to this day, almost seventy years later, I find the photograph quite poignant.

Return to Montego Bay: 1:00 AM, February 6th 1959.

In the photograph, my father is on the right as we look at it, looking happy. Until the end of his days, he was to regard this as one of the major achievements, not just of his time as Head of External Finance but of his entire career; it occurred on his thirty-fourth birthday. Next to him is his boss, Finance Minister the Hon Noel Nethersole.

On Mr Nethersole's right is the man who had recruited my father to Jamaica, Financial Secretary the Hon E.R. Richardson, and on Mr Richardson's right is the Solicitor-General, the Hon Ewart Forrest.

This proved to be one of the last photographs taken of the Minister. A little more than a month later, he died suddenly and unexpectedly at the age of fifty-five. So passed, long before his time, one of the finest statesmen ever to dedicate his life to the public service of Jamaica and her citizens.

My father recorded in his 1983 memoir that,

> *"On March 17th 1959, my Minister and good friend Crab Nethersole died of a heart attack. On the 21st we went to Crab's State funeral. On the 22nd I had a small farewell do in the Ministry to which Norman Manley came and said kind words; on March 23rd we boarded the Reina del Mar and took our leave of Jamaica."*[xliv]

My father relates how my mother, much though she enjoyed her time in Jamaica, was homesick and keen to return to Wales. It seems that my father decided more or less immediately after Mr Nethersole's death that, having completed the negotiation of the Wall Street Bond, there was little more for him to do in Kingston, and his heart had gone out of the job following the loss of his ministerial chief.

The day after Mr Nethersole died, the *Kingston Gleaner* said he had been

> *"wholly responsible for the ideas behind the work of transforming Jamaica's financial institutions from the pattern of Crown Colony administration into the modern machinery of a self-governing nation which it is now becoming."*

Although the Bank of Jamaica was formally founded two years after his death, on May 1st 1961, Mr Nethersole is regarded as the Father of the Bank, and his statue stands as a permanent memorial to him at the front of the Bank's headquarters in Nethersole Place, Kingston.

The foundation of the bank coincided with the publication of *Capital Funds in Underdeveloped Countries*[xlv], which my father dedicated to Mr Nethersole and which, when its copyright expired in 2021, came into the public domain in the USA and

> *"was selected by scholars as being culturally important and part of the knowledge base of civilization as we know it."*

Following the expiry of the copyright, this notice continued,

> *"within the United States, you may freely copy and distribute this work. Scholars believe, and we concur, that this work is important enough to be preserved, reproduced, and made generally available to the public."*

This description makes it sound as though the book is largely of historic interest. It is my contention that, on the contrary, the analysis of *Capital Funds* is still highly relevant today.

****

The central theme of *Capital Funds* is the paramount role that a Central Bank should play in an emerging economy. It sets out a blueprint of what its functions should be and how they could be carried out in order to fulfil this role.

In the Foreword to the book, my father was careful to state that the views expressed in it were his and should not be attributed to any third person, writing that,

> *"My interest in the subject matter of this essay was much stimulated by my experience during the years 1957 to 1959.....It is therefore considerably more than mere formality for me to emphasise upon the reader the wholly personal nature of the views expressed in the pages which follow. In no sense should they be taken as necessarily reflecting the opinion or policy of the present government of that country or any of its predecessors."*[xlvi]

Notwithstanding this disclaimer, it is my conviction that the ideas set out in *Capital Funds* very much reflect the discussions he had with the Minister during that period and Mr Nethersole's vision for a future Jamaican Central Bank. However, unfortunately, in 1961 it was not possible for my father to confer with his former boss on this matter, so quite rightly he absolved the man to whom he dedicated the book from any responsibility for its content.

Running to just five chapters and 104 pages, it opens with a statement of its mission, which is

> *"designing financial institutions and relationships to maximise the contribution which can be made (to economic development) by domestic financial resources."*

Its emphasis is thus on mobilising domestic, rather than foreign, capital. This is reinforced by a concern that any foreign loans would need to be repaid in foreign currency, potentially placing strain on its Balance of Payments, which the mobilisation of domestic sources of finance would avoid.

The first chapter of the book, entitled 'The Currency System', advocates the repatriation of a nation's currency reserves from the metropolitan centre following its independence, with the reserves managed instead by a newly created Central Bank.

The second chapter, 'The Role of Central Banks', begins conventionally enough, with their core functions being

> *"the administration of the money supply and the regulation of an adequate structure of credit institutions in the economy."*

These functions are no different from those of a central bank in a developed country, such as the Bank of England or the American Federal Reserve. However, on page 27, a radical extension of a Central Bank's functions is proposed, namely,

> *"the financing of long-term development within the economy....(and) active and positive encouragement of the growth of local capital and money markets."*

The third chapter, 'Commercial Banking', considers what this approach would imply for a Central Bank's relationship with commercial banks within its territory. Under the colonial system, the lending policies of commercial banks were determined by their Head Offices, "primarily with regard to monetary conditions prevailing in the country in which the Head Office was situated." *Capital Funds* concluded that this is not necessarily wholly negative for a colony, as it could result in lower interest rates and perhaps greater capital availability than under full independence. However, its overall conclusion is that treating commercial banks in their colonies as no different from local branches in the metropolitan country would, on balance, have negative consequences for colonies, because

> *"their economic growth could not hope to prosper, so long as the flow of credit to them ebbs and flows in sympathy with conditions prevailing in distant, and very different, metropolitan areas."* [xlvii]

A further disadvantage of the colonial system was that, in practice, commercial banks lent primarily to expatriate companies, "usually those involved in the cultivation and export of primary products", for relatively short periods. Overdrafts and one-year loans for working capital purposes were available; loans for longer-term investment projects were not.

The colonial system also drained funds from the colonies back to the metropolitan centre, rather than recycling them for lending within the country itself. *Capital Funds* noted that,

> *"At the end of 1954, more than thirty per cent of the funds collected by commercial banks over the British colonies as a whole were remitted out of the colonial territories, almost wholly to London head offices or the money market. By the end of 1959, the proportion had fallen to a little over twenty per cent....Although the drain of new funds from poor to rich through the banking system has fallen in recent years, the colonies remain net losers."*[xlviii]

This net loss could be reduced after independence through the creation of nationally owned commercial banks under the supervision of the Central Bank. The Central Bank could use the regulatory tools at its disposal to encourage a gradual shift in bank lending from expatriate companies exporting to the metropolitan country towards domestic enterprise.

> *"Independent policy implies a programme of development for agriculture and industry, designed to provide for the needs of the whole population rather than those of an imperial power."* [xlix]

The book's fourth chapter, 'The Creation of Lending Institutions', recognised the fragility of the financial system in most newly independent countries, and considered how the Central Bank could help to address this issue. It concluded that the Central Bank, so far from adopting a largely supervisory role as in developed economies such as the UK and USA, should play an active role in creating entirely new financial institutions such as investment trusts:

> *"The placing of funds in an investment trust, for example, enables holders of small amounts of capital to distribute their funds over a wide range of industries and enterprises, and this distribution achieves a significant reduction of the risk to which capital is exposed in the course of investment."*[l]

This role would help address the challenge highlighted in *Capital Funds*:

> *"The poorer a country is, the greater the need for agencies to collect and invest the savings of the broad mass of persons and institutions within its borders; yet given the high degree of risk inherent in investment in a poor country, it may prove essential that the institutions established to collect and invest the savings of the community should be supported by a guarantee of its government."*[li]

The role of Central Bank envisaged by this blueprint would thus extend well beyond regulating commercial banks and providing them with emergency funds. Under the Jamaican model, the Central Bank would be proactive in developing financial institutions and capital markets. In addition to investment trusts, *Capital Funds* suggests that the Central Bank could assist in creating intermediaries such as building societies, agricultural credit banks, and development finance companies, staffed by individuals with specialist training and expertise in these fields.

****

Over the years since *Capital Funds* was first published, the governments of many emerging countries have established development finance companies (DFCs) able to take permanent equity (normally a minority stake) in companies, and willing to lend for much longer terms than commercial banks.

Some thirty years after the publication of *Capital Funds*, I drew on my experience as a Loan Officer with the European Investment Bank to analyse the performance of twenty-five DFCs in sub-Saharan Africa[lii]. The practical problem that the EIB faced was that it could not lend directly to small- and medium-sized enterprises in Africa because its administrative costs in undertaking the appropriate due diligence would be prohibitively high, as described in Appendix 2. The solution devised to address this problem was to provide credit lines to national DFCs for them to on-lend to small- and medium-sized enterprises.

During the 1970s and 1980s, the EIB often played an active role in setting up DFCs, in collaboration with other international development finance institutions such as the International Finance Corporation (IFC). However, by the late 1980s, an increasing number of DFCs were experiencing financial problems, often caused by the fact that, while the EIB lent in ECU – precursor to the Euro – the DFCs would on-lend in their national currencies. The

EIB stipulated the maximum on-lending margin which the DFC was allowed to charge, which varied between four and eight per cent, and was inadequate to cover the foreign-exchange losses which many DFCs suffered. Of the twenty-five national DFCs covered in my analysis, less than half a dozen were rated as financially stable in the mid-1980s.

A central recommendation of my 1992 paper was therefore that international development finance institutions such as the EIB and IFC should take steps to minimise the exposure of African DFCs to foreign exchange losses, for example by investing in DFC equity. The 1992 analysis found that DFCs whose shareholders included international development finance institutions performed better than those that were wholly-owned by national governments.

International institutions could work alongside DFCs and Central Banks to develop their national Stock Markets. This follows a recommendation of the final chapter of *Capital Funds*, entitled 'The Development of Capital Markets', advocating active Central Bank sponsorship of national capital markets, commenting that,

> *"Capital (in developing countries) is not only scarce, but often used in ways which are not conducive to the maximum rate of economic expansion. A good deal of capital has been remitted out of under-developed territories in the past and invested in international financial centres where safety and liquidity are secured, but where the need for capital*

is considerably less pressing than in the territories from which the funds came." [liii]

Capital Funds suggested that a national securities exchange be developed in phases. The first phase would entail the creation of a market in short-term Treasury Bills, offered by tender by the Central Bank and redeemable ninety days after issue. In the second phase, the government would offer longer term government bonds for sale, and in the third phase a Stock Exchange would be set up for initial public offers (IPOs) of company shares. In the fourth phase, a secondary market would develop in quoted shares following their IPO.

Although *Capital Funds* was published more than sixty years ago, the Central Bank model it proposed remains relevant today in addressing the challenges faced by many countries in Africa, South Asia, Latin America, the Caribbean and the Pacific Islands – territories with fragile capital markets whose combined population, of some four billion people, comprises over half of the world's total population.

The political vision which inspired the Central Bank model set out in *Capital Funds* was that of the Jamaican Finance Minister of the late 1950s. It therefore seems appropriate to conclude this chapter with the dedication to him on the first page of the book:

Respectfully dedicated to the memory of
NOEL NETHERSOLE
Good friend;
Tolerant master;
Faithful servant of his people.

5 The End of the Keynesian Era

Just a few days after the State Funeral of the Hon Noel Newton Nethersole in Jamaica, we were on our way back to Britain, on board the *Reina del Mar*, bound for Liverpool out of Kingston. A few weeks later we were met by my grandfather and Uncle Bernie when we disembarked at the Port of Liverpool, and drove back to Wales – first to Pembroke Dock, and then to our house, Eryl Mor, in Aberystwyth, where my father resumed his academic career at the University College more or less where he had left off.

Life on the Ocean Wave: a children's party on board the *Reina del Mar*, April 1959.

From left to right as we look at the photo: my sisters Mary, Christine and Tessa, with me behind Tessa and somewhat overshadowed by her. Plus ça change…

I began my own academic career at the Park Avenue Primary School Aberystwyth on September 8th 1959. A little less than a year later in August 1960 the final member of the family arrived in the shape of my younger brother Philip. For a time, it seemed that he might not be long for the world, as he could not keep his food down, and the Aberystwyth medics completely failed to diagnose the problem, let alone devise an effective prognosis. At one point in October they came up with the conclusion that he was suffering from a hernia and recommended surgery. Meanwhile, Philip's weight dropped to dangerously low levels. "Finally," my father reported in his memoir, "through my unofficial resort to the university medical people, he was taken to Llandough Hospital to meet a real physician and immediately operated on for pyrolic stenosis."

Fortunately, the intervention was just in time and Philip recovered. In her diary, my mother recorded that, on January 19th 1961, Philip was weighed and discovered to have gained nearly 3 lbs in five weeks. Many years later, my father revealed to me that the "real physician" at Llandough Hospital had been Jewish, and in his opinion had been held back in his career by anti-Jewish prejudice.

At about the same time as Philip's early health crisis, my father felt that his own career was being held back by age prejudice, when Professor Beacham's recommendation that he be promoted to Senior Lecturer was rejected on the grounds that he was far too young. The result was that, in March 1961, we were on the new move again, this time to Dublin, where my father took up the post of Deputy Director at the newly created Irish Economic Research Institute (ERI). While there, he authored eight ERI research papers, including the very first that the Institute published, entitled 'The ownership of personal property in Ireland' (October 1961), and the eleventh in the series, in which he returned to his old stamping ground of the National Debt, entitled 'Public debt and economic development'.

Shortly after the publication of the first ERI paper my grandfather died suddenly in December 1961. By a cruel twist of fate, the cause of death was a massive heart attack, as in the case of Noel Nethersole in 1959. My father was quite a self-controlled man, not given to displays of emotion, but I could see when the news came that he was quite shaken. After he had left to get the first flight from Dublin back to Wales for the funeral, I asked my mother what had happened. She said that she thought my grandfather's heart had been weak ever since he had been gassed on the Somme many years before, and perhaps the truth was, not that we should be sad that he had died, but happy that he had lived as long as he had. Her account, more than sixty years ago, was confirmed by an contemporaneous Obituary Notice in the Pembrokeshire local press, which reported that,

> *"Only his closest friends realised there were times when the effects of the poisonous mist which rolled over the Flanders battlefield so many years before were with him still and causing him great distress."*[liv]

The Notice went on,

> *"He was proud of the Council's achievements in bringing to the town a standard of illumination which bears comparison with any in the country. In view of his great work in this and other fields, the epitaph 'He strove for light' would not be inappropriate."*

The street lights, reminiscent of the *Bel Epoque* style of his youth at the turn of the 19th and 20th centuries, still stand on Dimond Street. If inter-planted with palm trees – should there exist a species that could withstand harsh winters – then Pembroke Dock's high street could yet transformed into the most elegant boulevard in Wales.

My grandfather's obituary concluded by reporting that, on the morning of his funeral, flags flew at half-mast at the Municipal Office, the British Legion Hall, and the Trades and Labour Hall, "where Mr Nevin was much respected for his work in the Socialist cause and as chairman for many years of the local branch of the Transport and General Workers' Union."

****

Our sojourn in Dublin came to an end when my father was appointed to a Chair in Economics at the University College of Wales in Aberystwyth at the age of thirty-eight, a remarkably young age at a time when just one-in-twenty of the school population went on to university and the average age of a university professor was closer to sixty than to forty.

My father's early appointment was the consequence of both forces that Machiavelli says shape our destiny – *Fortuna* and *Vertu*.

Fortuna because he had the good luck that a vacancy was open at the University College of Wales in Aberystwyth, which he had attended as an undergraduate, postgraduate, and lecturer, and where he had a friend at court in the form of the departmental head, Professor Arthur Beacham, with whom he had worked for many years, and whom he liked and respected.

Vertu because he was a known quantity, a capable lecturer with a growing academic reputation. He had already published more than forty academic papers and four books. The first of these, *The Problem of the National Debt*, was perhaps largely forgotten by 1963, as the problem that book sought to address – the scale of the UK's National Debt and the burden it placed on public finances – was regarded as having been largely solved by 1963. However, his second book, *The Mechanism of Cheap Money*, was by that time, seven years after its first publication, recognised as an authoritative work on British monetary policy during the 1930s. *Capital Funds in Underdeveloped Countries* had also received a favourable reception on its English publication in 1961, and by 1963 had been translated into Spanish and Japanese.

Though both the *Mechanism of Cheap Money* and *Capital Funds* had been well received within the specialist communities to which they were addressed, neither was exactly a best-seller. However, his *Textbook of Economic Analysis*, based on lecture notes and first published in

1958, was beginning to sell steadily as a popular introductory text to economics.

The Young Professor, 1963.

A photograph of my father at the time of his appointment to a Chair in the Department of Economics at the University College of Wales, Aberystwyth, in 1963

So our gypsy-like existence came to an end. In being appointed to the Chair of Economics at the University College of Wales in Aberystwyth, my father had achieved his ambition, and he and my mother were to make only one further move during their lifetimes, when we moved to Swansea in 1968.

Prior to his appointment as a Professor of Economics, my father's research had been largely empirical in nature, based on statistics and historical analysis rather than the application of mathematical methods, which were becoming increasingly popular following the publication of Paul Samuelson's *Economics.* First published in 1948, Samuelson's *Economics* subsequently ran to nineteen editions and was probably the most important influence on the approach taken to the subject during the final half of the 20th century. It was translated into more than forty languages and sold over four million copies. *Economics* popularised the neoclassical synthesis first developed by John Hicks – the same economist who recommended my father for his Jamaican posting – in a seminal 1937 paper, 'Mr Keynes and the Classics'[lv]. This paper formalised Keynes' *General Theory* in mathematical terms and helped to bring it into mainstream economics, a process completed by Samuelson's *Economics.*

Some thirty years after his 1937 paper, Sir John Hicks paid a visit to our house in Aberystwyth. As this was the first and only time I ever met a future Nobel prize winner in the kitchen of my home, I am somewhat embarrassed to report that he was so diffident and unassuming that he made very little impression on me, and that, beyond the customary greetings, I didn't say a word to him. In my defence, I was only about twelve years old at the time and yet to commence my study of economics, let alone appreciate the elegance of the IS-LM analysis that underpinned his neoclassical synthesis. Suffice it to say that, on the evidence of our fleeting acquaintance, I am not surprised that it was not he, as the man who first developed the synthesis, who went on to become a super-star and multi-millionaire, but the man who popularised it, Paul Samuelson.

Samuelson's *Economics* helped to disseminate macro-economics, the study of the economy as a whole, and Keynesian methods for measuring and analysing it. At Aberystwyth, my father applied these methods in research undertaken with two young lecturers, Alan Roe and Jeff Round, to prepare estimates of the value and structure of the Welsh economy[lvi]. It was shortly after the publication of *The Structure of the Welsh Economy* that an eminent visitor arrived at our modest abode on Penglais Road.

Gwynfor Evans was at that time the President of Plaid Cymru, the Welsh National Party, and had just become the Party's first Member of Parliament, having scored a famous victory at the 1966 Carmarthen by-election. I recall him as a softly spoken man with silver grey hair and gentle eyes, whose kindly appearance hardly suggested an individual naturally cut out for the rough-and-tumble of politics. One suspects that what may have attracted him to the Welsh national cause was not any rigorous cost-benefit analysis of the economic impact of independence but rather an emotional attachment to the distinct language, culture, and religions of Wales, and one of the great achievements of his political career was the creation of a Welsh-speaking television channel. My guess is that his visit to my father was stimulated by a desire to enhance his understanding of the Welsh economy, on which my father was now an acknowledged expert, and perhaps also to ask my father's opinion as to whether Wales could prosper if it gained political independence from England. If so, based on his published work on the Welsh economy, I would imagine that my father's response would have been to confirm that Wales could indeed survive and perhaps thrive as an independent country, but would be well advised to maintain free-trade with her main partner, England, and seek to minimise non-tariff barriers between the two by avoiding the introduction of separate laws applying to business and commerce.

****

During his time as a Professor of Economics in Aberystwyth, between 1963 and 1968, there was a distinct shift in his research interests, from monetary issues to the Welsh economy and regional policy, on which he published sixteen articles and papers in addition to the jointly authored *Structure of the Welsh Economy*. As an independent non-political academic and a leading authority on Wales's economy at that time, he was increasingly called upon to offer opinions on Welsh economic affairs by the BBC and the *Western Mail,* the national Welsh newspaper. However, he did publish one final book on finance and banking, in the form of *The London Clearing Banks*, published by Elek in 1970 as part of their *Monographs on British Financial Institutions* series. This was co-authored with E.W. Davis, a researcher at the college.

I remember Mr Davis quite well, as he volunteered – or perhaps more accurately was press-ganged – into rescuing me from a remote village somewhere in the mountains of Cader Idris when I managed to lose touch with the rest of an Ardwyn group taken there on a walking tour during the annual school trip towards the end of the 1968 summer term. Cut off from the rest of civilisation, I made my way down the mountain and eventually found my way to a remote village with a single telephone box, from which I was able to call home and identify where I was. Ted Davis was deputed to find me and get me home, something of an imposition to put it mildly, but to his credit he took it in good heart and we enjoyed a pleasant enough conversation on the drive back to Aberystwyth.

Apparently, I was not the only pupil to have got lost that day in the mists of Cader Idris, for the following morning at the school assembly the headmaster, whom I remember only by his moniker of Dai Ball, read out a muster roll of a few other miscreants. The driver of the school coach had apparently waited for us to appear for some time in vain, holding up everyone's return home, before putting out a general police call. Seated at the back of the assembly hall, I kept my head well down as the headmaster spoke, and wished in vain for a hole to open up and swallow me. Only after assembly was over did I discover that the adventure had considerably enhanced my reputation among my peers as a devil-may-care adventurer, rather like Steve McQueen in *The Great Escape*, although of course without the motorbike.

****

Unlike my father's earlier books, *The London Clearing Banks* was not a work of economic analysis nor an exposition of economic theory. It is more accurately categorised as a work of economic history, describing the development of the British banking system from the early days of the goldsmiths, though their metamorphosis into unlimited partnerships and country banks that proved in many cases to be financially unstable, into the development of joint-stock companies with limited liability that progressively consolidated into the 'Big Five' English clearing banks – in alphabetical order, Barclays, Lloyds, Midland, National Provincial and the Westminster Bank. By the interwar period, the Big Five controlled more than eighty per cent of all retail bank deposits in England and Wales, while the 'Big Two' Scottish banks – the Bank of Scotland and the Royal Bank of Scotland – enjoyed similar dominance north of the border.

The structure had evolved over the centuries into a cosy oligopoly. It had one major disadvantage – lack of competition offering genuine choice, so that bank customers often remained with same bank throughout their working lives. Against this, the banking structure in 1970 had one major advantage – stability – because none of the large clearing banks had an interest in rocking the boat by aggressive price-cutting. It was a comfortable existence, and the banks were, by later standards, very cautiously run. According to the *London Clearing Banks*, in 1969 they held eight per cent of their assets in cash, and their total liquidity, comprising cash and assets which could be quickly converted into cash such as Treasury Bills, represented thirty per cent of their assets. Their profit margin per branch in 1966 represented approximately two per cent of their deposits.[lvii]

Looking back on those bygone days more than half a century ago, it is notable how the textbooks of the time, including *The Textbook of Economic Analysis,* followed the convention of *The London Clearing Banks* in describing the role of commercial banks within the economic system without analysing their inner workings or regarding them as a source of potential instability. The period in the 18th and 19th centuries when banking collapses could plunge the entire economy into recession seemed to be over. The role of the banks was regarded as acting as passive middlemen between their depositors on the one hand, and their borrowers on the other, earning a steady profit from the margin they earned between the interest paid on deposits and the interest charged on loans.

In Keynes's analysis, the cause of the Great Depression of the 1930s was lack of confidence among investors, rather than any shortage of bank credit. His *General Theory* did not identify the banks themselves as a potential source of economic instability. His principal concern was the high level of unemployment at the time the *General Theory* was published, rather than the rate of inflation.

However, by the late 1960s, the principal economic challenge was rising inflation, which the Keynesian orthodoxy of the day failed to address. "The only relevant test of the validity of a hypothesis," wrote Milton Friedman in *Essays in Positive Economics* in 1953, "is comparison of prediction with experience." By the late

1960s, Friedman was leading a Monetarist Counter-Revolution which challenged the Keynesian orthodoxy of the day. Monetarist theory contended that a central tenet of Keynesian economics – that full employment could be achieved by higher government spending without inflationary consequences – was not borne out by experience. The Monetarist thesis was that there is a 'natural' rate of unemployment, and if a government sought to reduce unemployment below this natural rate by increasing government spending it would lead to higher inflation. In order to rein back inflation, the Monetarist School advocated tighter control of government spending and lower growth of the money supply.

As a young postgraduate student in Cambridge, my father had not been a fully paid-up member of the Keynesian School. Twenty years later, he followed the debate between the Keynesian and Monetarist Schools with an open mind. In 1970, the final chapter of *The London Clearing Banks* concluded with a section entitled 'The Revival of the Quantity Theory of Money.' His view at that time was that the efforts of post-Keynesian policymakers to apply "command and control" techniques to bring down inflation through prices and incomes policies directly limiting price and wage increases were fundamentally flawed. They caused significant distortions in the workings of the British economy and industrial unrest, and they ultimately failed because they did not address the growth in money supply that was the underlying cause of inflation.

I echoed this view in *The Age of Illusions*[lviii] and in a series of three articles published in the *Western Mail* between

March 5th and March 7th 1985. The first of these, 'How we lost a Golden Age'[lix], looked back fondly to the Keynesian era, and perhaps to my own childhood.

> *"The Keynesian era in economic policy between the 1940s and 1960s was something of a Golden Age. The rate of unemployment in Britain never rose above three per cent, or half a million people. Between 1953 in 1968, the rate of inflation never exceeded five per cent. The economy grew every year in real terms, by an average of almost three per cent. The British economy was in dynamic equilibrium. It was becoming steadily more prosperous. It was generating new jobs for school leavers and they had the prospect of rising real incomes as they got older. This was a solid basis on which they could build their homes and families."*

So where had it all gone wrong?

> *"The inflation which upset the post-war Golden Age was not caused by militant trade unions. It therefore could not be cured by incomes policies, trade union reforms, or any of the other labour market nostrums peddled by the Wilson and Heath Governments of the late 1960s and early 1970s. It was an international monetary inflation, which originated in the United States, but affected all Western economies. It was generated principally by the Vietnam War and the massive increase in military spending associated with it. The war resulted in a widening American budget deficit and an upsurge in the volume of American dollars on*

the world's money markets. The consequences were inevitable: an international inflation and the devaluation of the American dollar in the early 1970s, which destroyed the Bretton Woods system of fixed exchange rates. It also led to a commodity price explosion, seen most dramatically in the case of oil."[lx]

****

Against this turbulent background, family life went on. There is a photograph of a family wedding in Leamington Spa in July 1967 showing almost all the children and grandchildren of William Nevin, late Mayor of the Borough of Pembroke, looking rather happier and more prosperous than the family group gathered around Thomas and Honora Nevin on the occasion of their Golden Wedding Anniversary some forty years earlier.

A Family Wedding, Leamington Spa, July 1967.

[From left to right as we look at the photo (and their relationship to me) stood Dawn Nevin (cousin), Doreen Wren (aunt), my mother, myself, Tom McNally (uncle), Patricia Wren (cousin), Moira Wren (cousin), Philip Nevin (brother), Aubrey Wren (uncle) Pam and David Nevin (cousins), Peter Deakin and Angela Deakin née Nevin (bride and groom, cousins), Mark, Antoinette and Bernadette Nevin standing in front of the bride and groom (cousins), Yvonne and Bernard Nevin (aunt and uncle), Martin Nevin (cousin), Mary Helen Nevin (grandmother), Adrian Nevin (cousin), my father, Eileen McNally (aunt), Christine Nevin (sister) and Jonathan Wren (cousin)].

****

In 1968, my father was appointed to the Chair of Economics at the University College of Swansea, thus becoming Head of Department in his own right, rather than serving as the number two as he had in Aberystwyth

In the summer of 1968, we drove down from Aberystwyth to Swansea, an exercise that took an entire day. When the plan for the move was laid out over the kitchen table in Aberystwyth, I asked why the journey would take so long. "After all, Aberystwyth is only seventy miles from Swansea the crow flies."

"Yes, but we don't normally fly by crow," my father responded. A reply which my brother Paul, for reasons best known to himself, found utterly hilarious. I, on the other hand, didn't find his riposte was quite so amusing.

6 Textbook Economic Analysis

Now in his early forties, my father was at the peak of his career when he arrived in Swansea in 1968. *The Textbook of Economic Analysis* was selling well, and became the standard text for A-level students in Wales – indeed it was the textbook that I used when studying for my A-levels in the early Seventies. He also earned fees from broadcasting and journalism, which flourished in part due to the fact that it was easier to reach Cardiff and London from Swansea than from Aberystwyth. In the early 1970s, he was asked to advise the Police Federation of England and Wales in their pay negotiations with the Home Office. On accepting the appointment, he agreed an annual fee equivalent to the pay of a Police Constable. The royalties and fees he received from these sources were a more than useful supplement to his academic salary, generating annual revenues of approximately £6,000 in the early 1970s, equivalent to approximately £100,000 in 2024/25 prices. After allowing for the expenses incurred in carrying out this work and paying the costs of a university education for each of his children, they were sufficient to enable him to run a Jaguar motor car, in those days a much sought after status symbol.

It therefore seems rather curious that his inaugural lecture at the University College of Swansea delivered in February 1969, *Economics: Waiting for Godot*[lxi] struck a downbeat, even pessimistic, note regarding the outlook for Economics.

The lecture begins with the observation that, although for the first time a professional economist resided at 10 Downing Street, in the form of Labour Prime Minister Harold Wilson, and the civil service employed more economists than ever before, the reputation of the economics profession had never been lower. He then went on to provide a qualified, if somewhat sardonic, defence of his subject.

> *"A good deal of the catastrophic decline in the public reputation of our subject is less than just. Our system of government rests on the principle that decisions are taken by Ministers, not their advisers. A certain course of action can therefore never be taken to imply the presentation of expert advice of a similar nature; advice may not in fact have been sought on the issue in question nor, if sought, have been adopted in whole or even in part. Anyone who believes, as a matter of faith, that British politicians or their most senior officials are invariably guided by the best technical advice available to them must have been miraculously preserved from actual contact with those gentleman in the flesh."* [lxii]

He then went on to consider why the study of Economics had not realised the high expectations many had for it in the optimistic days of the Keynesian Revolution.

> *"What, then, are the fundamental causes of failure? Curiously enough, there seems to be general agreement on this. First, it is clear that the obsession amongst British economists with broad*

macroeconomic issues has led us to attempt judgements on problems involving a complexity of forces far beyond our present competence to handle; having mastered a few strokes of the doggy paddle, we have foolishly thrown ourselves in at the deepest of ends……This is partly due to the impact of the dazzling flash of intuition associated with the name of Maynard Keynes and which we have been ingenuous enough to label the Keynesian Revolution. The brilliant intellectual insight of Keynes, set against the broadest and most general backcloth of principle, was one thing; its detailed practical application to particular contexts and solutions of particular problems is, alas, quite another."[lxiii]

The conclusion of *Waiting for Godot* was that Economics should cease its quest for all-embracing solutions to the world's problems, and instead limit its ambitions.

> *"The future health of our subject depends on our willingness to redefine its scope, not in terms of the grand vistas over which we would like to imagine ourselves presiding in some ideal world, but of the area within which we are likely to be competent to reach something approaching scientific conclusions."*[lxiv]

It suggested that the achievement of this goal would be assisted by greater use of mathematical techniques and econometric analysis to analyse specific micro-economic problems.

My father was to apply this approach in his own work after 1970.

In the summer of 1970, Christine, Philip and I accompanied our parents on a trip to Canada and the USA. My father had a one-month teaching appointment at the Queens University, Ontario, who housed us in a wooden cabin by the shore of Lake Loughborough. After a month at Lake Loughborough, we travelled down to St Pauls / Minneapolis, where, my father's memoir recalls, he was carrying out "some small piece of work for the Federal Bank of Minneapolis" for a week. This was followed by a touring holiday staying in various Howard Johnson motels in the northern USA, visiting the Gettysburg battlefield and suchlike, before driving back to New York and flying home to Swansea at the end of August.

"Throwing ourselves in at the deepest of ends"

Me diving into Lake Loughborough during our stay there in July 1970 with Christine in the boat watching on.

It was while we were in Canada that I conceived the ambition of getting a place at Oxford University to study philosophy, politics and economics. At the time, it seemed like a forlorn hope. Although Oxford's approach to economics was based more on economic history and case studies than Cambridge, the minimum qualifications for entrance included a Maths 'O' Level. My prospects for achieving this seemed remote, as I regularly posted scores of twenty per cent or less in Maths school exams.

A Moment Captured in Time

Lake Loughborough, Canada, July 1970: Philip climbing aboard, Christine enjoying a swim, me in the boat.

My problem with Maths related not so much to Arithmetic – I could just about work out how long it would take to fill a bath of water if provided with information about the rate of water flow and the capacity of the bath – but to the more abstract subjects of Algebra, Geometry and

Trigonometry, which were all Greek to me. In fact, I found Greek a lot easier.

The solution I devised to my Maths problem was to invest in Teach Yourself books covering the subjects with which I was struggling, and to work my way through them, painstakingly, at a pace I was happy with – i.e. very slowly – completing the tests at the end of each chapter to confirm I had understood it correctly, or, if not, going over it again. While it would be an exaggeration to say that I succeeded in mastering any of the subjects so addressed, at least I comprehended them well enough to achieve the requisite fifty per cent pass mark. My results in the mock 'O' Levels of the Spring of 1971 were sufficiently good to convince me that I had at least an outside chance of scraping through the Oxford Entrance Exam the following year.

The day I completed the mock 'O' Levels I took the Number 77 bus to Limseslade. For some reason I had missed the usual school bus which stopped at the top of Rotherslade Road where we lived, so instead had to walk over the cliff path from Limseslade to Rotherslade. It was getting dark and the path was completely deserted. The wind was blowing a fierce gale and waves were crashing onto the rocks, sending spray onto the path where I stood. As I stopped to gaze at the fury below, I felt an absolute conviction that I would succeed in my ambition. Arriving home, I sat down in our warm sitting room with a cup of tea and listened to Rimsky-Korsakov's *Capriccio Espagnol*, safely sheltered from the storm outside. To this day, whenever I hear the *Capriccio Espagnol*, I feel a surge of optimism and wellbeing.

An Epiphany, April 1971

Gareth C. Thomas 1955-2019, "View from Rotherslade towards Limeslade" (Author's Collection).

In fact, the supreme confidence I felt during my walk from Limeslade to Rotherslade very nearly proved misplaced, but I did manage to scrape into Oxford as the humblest of commoners the following year, and took up a place at Pembroke College in the autumn of 1973, where I immediately succumbed to terrible homesickness and a yearning for home and the cliffs and sea I had left behind.

Still, it does go to show that, with a combination of confidence, dedication and determination, one can achieve the unlikeliest of ambitions.

****

It was not long after my cliff walk that a rather curious visitor arrived in our home in the form of Desmond Donnelly, who until a short time before had been the Member of Parliament for Pembroke. He had first won the Pembrokeshire seat for the Labour Party at the 1950 General Election, defeating the sitting Member, Gwilym Lloyd George. Major Lloyd George's absence from Parliament had, it may be recalled, denied my parents the opportunity to enter the visitor's gallery of House of Commons during their courtship in 1947 and witness great figures of the day like Churchill and Attlee in action.

Major Lloyd George suffered divine retribution when Desmond Donnelly, the Labour candidate, defeated him at the 1950 General Election with a winning majority of just 129 votes. It did not mark the end of Major Lloyd George's political career, however. Perhaps as a salute to his late father, the First World War Prime Minister David Lloyd George, who had been a close Cabinet ally during Asquith's reforming Liberal Government forty years earlier, Winston Churchill elevated the Major to the House of Lords, regaling in the title of 1st Viscount Tenby, and appointed him as Home Secretary in his final administration. Today the 1st Viscount Tenby is remembered, if at all, as the Home Secretary who failed to commute the death sentence of Ruth Ellis, the last woman to be hanged in Great Britain in July 1955.

Meanwhile, back in Pembrokeshire, Desmond Donnelly's conscientious work as the constituency MP was rewarded by steady increases in his Parliamentary majority at successive elections during the 1950s and 1960s. However, his rise within the Parliamentary Labour Party came to an abrupt end following the death of his mentor, Hugh Gaitskell, and his replacement as Labour leader by Harold Wilson in 1963. The story goes that Mr Donnelly took the precaution of writing letters to both of the main leadership candidates, Harold Wilson and George Brown, promising each of them his unswerving support. Unfortunately, he then made the mistake of putting the letter to Wilson in the envelope addressed to Brown and vice-versa. If true, this story would help to explain why he failed to gain any ministerial appointment after Harold Wilson became Prime Minister in 1964, despite his obvious credentials.

Denied ministerial preferment, Donnelly became an increasingly unreliable and erratic figure on the Labour backbenches. In alliance with another maverick Labour MP, Woodrow Wyatt, he publicly opposed Labour's policy of nationalising the steel industry. Since the Wilson Government of 1964-66 had only a tiny majority in Parliament, their opposition forced the postponement of the Steel Nationalisation Bill. It was only passed into law after the 1966 General Election when Labour secured a decisive majority.

By the late 1960s, Desmond Donnelly had gained a reputation as a troublemaker and any prospects he had of advancement within the Labour Party had long since evaporated. He resigned the Labour Party whip in the House of Commons in January 1968 and, not to be outdone, the Labour Party then expelled him from the Party altogether. The consequence was that he fought the

1970 General Election under the nominal banner of a newly formed 'Democratic Party'. The result was as follows:

Result of the 1970 General Election in the Constituency of Pembrokeshire.

Candidate	Party	Votes	%
Nicholas Edwards	Conservative	19,120	34.1%
Gordon Parry	Labour	17,889	31.9%
Desmond Donnelly	Democratic Party	11,824	21.1%
Wynne Samuel	Plaid Cymru	3,681	6.6%
David Wynford Thomas	Liberal	3,541	6.3%
	Total:	**56,055**	**100.0%**

Desmond Donnelly's achievement in gaining more than twenty per cent of the vote on his personal record running essentially as an independent was highly respectable. But in politics no-one wins a prize for being a good loser. While Nicholas Edwards went on to become Secretary of State for Wales in Mrs Thatcher's Government between 1979 and 1987 and was subsequently ennobled as Baron Crickhowell, and Gordon Parry became a much respected elder of the Welsh Labour Party, Desmond Donnelly's political career was at an end.

What he wished to discuss with my father when he arrived at our home not long after his election defeat I never did discover, as, unlike Harry Johnson, he seemed disinclined to pass the time of day with a sixteen-year-old. The only thing I did find out for sure was that the discussions he held with my father lasted well into the night and were generously lubricated by my father's whisky. If I were to hazard a guess on the subject of their conversation, it would be that Mr Donnelly might have been seeking my father's endorsement for some scheme to revive his political career. Since my father was always very careful to remain politically neutral, if this was what the erstwhile MP had hoped, he was to be disappointed.

By 1974, Desmond Donnelly was a man without a Party, without a faith, short of money following the failure of various ventures, and with only the shattered remnants of a once promising political career on which to reflect. It is recorded that he checked into a hotel room at West Drayton near Heathrow Airport on April 3rd 1974, where he ran a hot bath, drank a bottle of vodka and took a massive overdose of barbiturates. These tasks accomplished, he then slipped slowly into oblivion.

After his death, his erstwhile colleagues in the Labour Party were notable by their silence. It seemed that no one wished to be associated with the maverick former MP who had won the Pembrokeshire constituency for the Labour cause almost a quarter of a century earlier and served it well for twenty years thereafter.

No one, that is, apart from my father, who, in a letter to the *Western Mail*, recalled Desmond Donnelly with affection and admiration, expressing regret at his passing and concluding that "we shall not see his like again."

****

One reason for my father's regard for Mr Donnelly might have been that, in the fallen MP, he saw a fellow spirit who had suffered the consequences of expressing the truth as he saw it, however unpopular that might be.

Two years before Mr Donnelly's death, my father published two opinion pieces in the *Western Mail* at the time of the first miners' strike in early 1972[lxv]. The first of these, entitled 'Miners' battle against destiny is one they cannot win', opened with the ominous words that,

> *"If there was ever an industrial dispute which bore all the marks of a classical tragedy, moving with remorseless inevitability to a totally predictable bloodletting all round, this surely is it. The arguments being used on each side are eminently reasonable and convincing: they are also completely destructive of each other."*

The article continued,

> *"The miners argue, quite correctly, that from being at the top of the industrial league table they have slipped well down into its lower reaches; can anyone be either surprised at, or unsympathetic with, their accumulated resentment at this erosion of their relative position? If we lived in a world in which a man's pay was governed solely by what, in somebody's book, he deserved in some sense, there would surely be no argument whatsoever."*

However, the article went on to state, with the remorseless logic of the gloomy science, that,

"In the world of reality, a man will be paid, not according to the conditions of his work, but according to what you, the consumer or taxpayer, are willing to pay for what it produces."

The article pointed to the declining demand for coal, which would only be exacerbated by rising wages and costs.

The second article, entitled 'The price of coal could be your lost job'[lxvi] developed the analysis of the first by arguing that, if the coal industry's rising costs were funded by government subsidies rather than higher prices, then it would set a precedent for other trade union leaders to

"argue, with total conviction, that their members too are a special case. One cannot escape the fact that, in all the expressions of sympathy and solidarity, not a single trade union has indicated that in its future wage demands it will agree that any special concession to the miners will be never adduced in argument……which could lead to a resumption of the disastrous cost inflation of 1970, when costs in Britain rose by around eleven per cent in a single year."

The article concluded that,

"We may be gambling in this settlement not only with the future of the coal industry but with the prospect of seeing the triumph of full employment, as we knew it in the 1950s and 1960s, snatched away from us for many years to come."

This forecast proved prescient. The British coal industry went into terminal decline. The 1972 settlement did not finally resolve the issue of the miners' pay, and it was followed by further bitter strikes in 1974 and 1984-85. Across the wider economy, the full employment levels achieved during the previous two decades were lost as Britain mired in stagflation – the painful combination of a stagnating economy and high inflation.

However, it seems unlikely that my father's opinions went down well in the coalmining valleys of South Wales. It was notable that he kept his head well down and made no public comment during subsequent mining disputes. Perhaps he had found, to his cost, that at times discretion is the better part of valour.

****

A happier application of the mathematical methods that he had recommended in his Inaugural Lecture at Swansea in February 1969 came in his work for the Police Federation during the 1970s and 1980s. In *Waiting for Godot*, he had concluded that,

> *"The emphasis in our work, and more especially in our teaching, must shift a great distance away from the spurious, pretentious indulging in policy recommendations over vast political areas for which our present competence simply does not equip us, and towards much more rigorous and empirically better informed investigations of narrowly-defined topics and problems in which*

there is at least some prospect of modest success."[lxvii]

The "narrowly defined problem" which *The Pay of the Policeman*[lxviii] addressed was the level of pay necessary to secure sufficient numbers of properly qualified police officers. The method applied to do this was, the report stated, " an econometric analysis of the supply of recruits to, and their retention within, the police service of England and Wales" during the period between 1949 and 1973.

The report began with a review of previous reports on police pay. The first was the report prepared by a committee under Lord Desborough in 1919, which was followed by what *The Pay of Policemen* termed the 'Desborough Era' in police pay from 1920 to 1948. The second was the report of the committee constituted under Lord Oaksey in 1948, followed by the 'Oaksey Era' from 1949 to 1959. This in turn was succeeded by the 'Willink Era' of 1960–1974, following the report of a committee under Sir Henry Willink published in 1959.

In all cases, the reports were led by Judges and resulted in recommendations based on notions of what would be a "fair" level of pay – a notion to which my father had given short shrift in his commentary on the 1972 miners' strike. In all cases, the reports were followed by a hike in police pay which temporarily halted the loss of police officers from the service. And in all cases, subsequent increases in police pay lagged behind the increase in average industrial earnings, leading to problems in recruitment and retention. As *The Pay of the Policeman* pointed out with regard to the experience of the Willink era,

> *"In 1962, police strength was less than 5,000 below authorised establishment; by the end of 1972, strength was more than 11,000 below establishment."*[lxix]

In line with the approach recommended in his 1969 Swansea Inaugural Lecture, *The Pay of the Policeman* rejected earlier lawyer-led approaches based on the concept of a "fair rate for the job" in favour of an econometric approach to estimate the pay levels required to attain the number of police officers needed in the service. The analysis started by identifying the factors likely to influence decisions as to whether individuals wished to become police officers, and, once in service, whether to continue to serve. It then drew on historic data for each of the twenty-four years between 1949 and 1973 to measure the importance of each of these factors.

The report provided estimates for two equations. The first measured the factors driving the number of new recruits into the force. The second measured the factors driving the number of withdrawals from the force, whether as a consequence of retirement or resignation.

The analysis identified three main factors influencing recruitment and retention. The first was the rate of unemployment. The higher the rate of unemployment, the easier it was to recruit new officers and the lower the level of departures from the service. "The dole remains an excellent recruiting sergeant," the report drily observed. The second was the pay of a police officer relative to available alternatives as measured by a "relative pay index". The higher the pay of police officers compared to alternative jobs, the easier it was to recruit new officers and the lower the rate of departures from the service. The third factor was the size of the police cadet force. The higher the size of the cadet force in any one year, the greater the number of new recruits in the following year.

The report found that both the recruitment and withdrawal regressions had strong predictive power. It concluded by applying the regression results to forecast police numbers in the year following submission of the report.

The report and the negotiations that followed resulted in an agreement that significantly increased police pay, and my father continued to advise the Police Federation for several years thereafter. I remember meeting him and PC Lesley Knowles of the Police Federation for dinner in London during the early 1980s prior to a meeting they had with the Home Office and my departure to the Solomon Islands on a loan appraisal mission the following day. My father's work with the Federation was founded on the solid base that underpins any successful relationship between a client and a professional adviser: mutual respect, genuine value-added, reasonable remuneration, and the delivery of satisfactory results for the client.

The Pay of the Policeman marked, to the best of my knowledge, the first occasion on which econometric techniques were employed to help determine public sector pay rates. Its specific findings are now more than half a century old and of largely historic interest. However, the methodology applied in the report could equally be applied to help determine pay rates across other areas of public service, including firemen, teachers, doctors and nurses, prison officers, administrative civil servants or indeed government economists.

****

My father's career was now entering its final phase and his research publications were diminishing. The fifth and final edition of the *Textbook of Economic Analysis* was published in 1981. He continued to engage in public debate and was an enthusiastic public advocate of Britain's membership of the European Economic Community. His final book, published in 1990, was on *The Economics of Europe*[lxx].

It is a paradox that the administrative responsibilities of the head of a university department may leave less time for the original research on which their reputation was built than when they occupied more junior posts and were perhaps less qualified to conduct original research and to draw insightful conclusions from it.

The most significant factor restricting my father's contributions in the 1980s was the sudden death of my mother at home in 1983 from a massive stroke, at the age of fifty-five. I was at that time working at the European Investment Bank in Luxembourg, and remember one of my colleagues commenting, before I flew home for the funeral, that although the death was a terrible blow to those who loved her, it was perhaps not such a bad way to go, as she would have suffered no pain. At the time I thought his comments were a little insensitive, but now recognise the justice of them, although of course I wish my mother had lived a lot longer.

A Late Photo of my Mother, circa 1980.

My mother's death devastated my father, who never fully recovered from it. He was fortunate in marrying, a couple of years later, Pat Langdon, a family friend who provided him support and companionship during his final years and provided him with a loving home which, given his limitations in domestic matters, he would have scarcely been able to provide for himself.

My own career was progressing. I was married in 1986, and in 1989 Caroline gave birth to our son, Jamie.

"Good Times Never Seemed So Good."

Caroline and I in the West Indies, 1987

My father and Pat visited us shortly after Jamie's birth, and I noticed that my father seemed old for his age – he was just sixty-four at the time. Not long afterwards, he underwent a heart bypass operation, which was a success and provided the energy for a few more years.

My father's mother passed away at the ripe old age of ninety-five a few months after Jamie's birth. She attributed her long life in part to a tea maker she kept by her bedside, which automatically awoke her every morning with a fresh cup of tea to start the day.

I had a premonition that my father would not live to the advanced age of his mother when, during a walk with him in Greenwich Park one day, some bleak nihilistic words of Swinburne came to mind.

From too much love of living
From hope and fear set free,
We thank, with brief thanksgiving
Whatever gods may be
That no life lives forever;
That dead men rise up never;
That even the weariest river
Winds somewhere safe to sea.

He passed away in Singleton Hospital, Swansea, following complications after surgery on a stomach ulcer, on September 11th 1992 at the age of sixty-seven.

7 The Swansea School of Monetary Economics

My father's intellectual legacy, in the shape of his considerable body of published research and economic analysis over the years, does not exercise much influence today. Many of his academic papers address evanescent issues now of largely historic interest. His books are long out of print, and, although some can still be acquired second-hand or be found in a limited number of university libraries, are little read. Nevertheless, it is my submission that his ideas, and the ideas of other Welsh economists of his era and the two individuals who most influenced his thinking as a young man, Harry G. Johnson and Noel Nethersole – a disparate group whom I shall collectively refer to as the Swansea School of Monetary Economics – remain highly relevant today. The contrarian in me says that, even if they do not exercise much influence in the world's Finance Ministries and Central Banks, it may actually be of advantage to individual investors who can profit from the authorities' mistakes in monetary management.

The Swansea School is distinct from either the Monetarist School or the Keynesian School, although it draws on the insights of both. As developed by my father it has three central tenets: that money matters; that the competence of the Central Bank matters; and that the stability of the financial system also matters.

Money Matters

The Monetarist School is based on the premise that changes in the supply of money drive changes in inflation. "Inflation is always and everywhere a monetary phenomenon," as Milton Friedman said. The historical evidence set out in Appendix 1 throws some doubt on the strong version of the Quantity Theory, which posits that monetary growth can be used to precisely predict future price trends. On the other hand, British experience since 1900 suggests that rapid monetary growth during wartime (1914-1918 and 1939-1945) and peacetime (during the 1970s and 2020s) is followed by inflationary spikes with socially disruptive results. The evidence does not appear to be consistent with a counter hypothesis, advocated for example by Modern Monetary Theory, that sovereign governments can print as much money as they want without unduly worrying about rising levels of National Debt, provided they control the currency in which they borrow and so can always create more money to repay their debts. The advocates of Modern Monetary Theory recommend that, instead of using monetary policy to rein back inflation, if prices start to rise government spending should be reduced or taxes increased in order to curb aggregate demand.

Aristotle defined Virtue as the happy medium between two extremes. The Swansea School occupies such a position in rejecting the extreme versions of Modern Monetary Theory – that money doesn't much matter at all – and the Monetarist School – that money is all that matters in determining future inflation – and concludes that monetary growth is a useful predictor of future inflation. It can therefore be used with advantage in considering what investment positions to take. If monetary growth is well in excess of the real growth rate of an economy – in the case of the UK, if money is growing by more than four to five per cent a year – then prices are likely to rise in the near future, making fixed-income securities such as government bonds less attractive and signalling a shift into equity. If monetary growth is broadly in line with underlying economic growth plus a modest rate of inflation – in the case of the UK, if money supply is increasing between one and five per cent annually – then inflation is likely to remain low and stable, and there is no need for a significant change in the proportion of bonds and equities held in a balanced investment portfolio. However, if monetary growth is one per cent or less, and particularly if it is falling, then a reduction in future inflation is likely, and it may be a signal to reduce the proportion of an investment portfolio held in equities and increase the proportion held in bonds.

Investment analysts over the years have concluded that inflation is bad for bonds and comparatively good for equities, while deflation is bad for equities and good for bonds. However, rather than waiting for inflation or deflation to arrive, by which time bond and equity prices may have already moved, the advantage of monetary analysis is that it can serve as a tool to predict likely future inflation trends and therefore enable the astute investor to stay ahead of market movements.

The implication for Central Banks, as set out in Appendix 1, is that they should use the tools at their disposal to maintain a low and steady rate of monetary growth.

The Competence of the Central Bank Matters

"Competence" is used here in both senses of the word – both a Central Bank's area of competence, where it is qualified and authorised to act, and that it should do so with competence, or effectively and efficiently.

The Government's Bank

Going back to the origins of central banking in the 17th century, the primary role for which the Bank of England was incorporated in 1694 was to raise money on behalf of the King to fund his continental wars. It did so by issuing gilt-edged stock on the Government's behalf, bonds whose certificates were edged in gilt to emphasise that there were "as good as gold," and would be redeemed for gold.

This early public relations exercise worked, and British Governments were able to borrow long-term at interest rates of approximately 3½ per cent until the onset of high inflation during the 1960s. Even as this is written in the mid-2020s, long-term borrowing rates, at approximately 4½ per cent, are no higher than the rate of inflation.

It is a matter for the British Government, and in particular HM Treasury, to determine what the amount of Government borrowing should be, and to ensure that the National Debt is maintained at prudent levels, perhaps with a goal of reducing the National Debt to no more than sixty per cent of National Income, in line with the guidance of the 1992 Maastricht Treaty. Having received its political instructions, the Debt Management Office of the Bank of England appears to have done a competent job over the years in its day-to-day management of the National Debt, although, at the time of writing, the amount of debt outstanding, and particularly index-linked debt, appears worryingly high relative to the UK's National Income.

The Bankers' Bank

At the time of its incorporation, the Bank of England was given the right to issue banknotes convertible into gold on demand. During the 19th century dozens of banks in England and Scotland had the same right. However, over the years, the number of banks authorised to issue banknotes was progressively reduced. Many of them became insolvent when they were unable to convert their banknotes into gold on demand. Many others were acquired by larger banks as the sector consolidated and joint stock banks with limited liability gradually absorbed unlimited partnerships. After a series of banking crises, the Bank Charter Act of 1844 restricted the ability of commercial banks to issue notes, and in 1921 the Bank of England was formally granted a legal monopoly on issuing banknotes in England and Wales, although in Scotland the historic right to issue banknotes was retained by existing banks.

The Bank of England's privileged position as the sole authorised issuer of banknotes meant that it was the ultimate source of cash for commercial banks if additional funds were needed to fund their depositors' withdrawal requests. *The London Clearing Banks* reports that, during the first seventy years of the 20th century, UK clearing banks sought to minimise their reliance on the Bank of England by retaining ten per cent of their assets in cash and a further twenty per cent in liquid form such as Treasury Bills readily convertible into cash. These prudential ratios were abandoned after the liberalisation of the banking sector during the 1990s. The result was that commercial banks reduced their cash and liquid asset reserves to dangerously low levels, many became insolvent during the financial crisis of 2007–2009, and the Bank of England's function as "lender of last resort" was considerably extended to become "investor of last resort" as the British Government took over a number of banks in order to avoid a severe credit contraction and risk a second Great Depression.

The Central Banks' Bank

The third area of competence of a traditional Central Bank is the management of foreign exchange reserves. During the Gold Standard era, the Bank of England intervened to ensure the convertibility of Sterling into gold at a fixed rate. After the collapse of the Gold Standard in the early 1930s, the Bank of England set up an Exchange Equalisation Account to manage gold and foreign currency reserves and minimise fluctuations in the external value of Sterling. This continued through the Bretton Woods era.

Thus, under what might be termed the Anglo-Saxon model, a modern central bank has three core competences. The first is to manage the Government's borrowing programme and management of the National Debt. The second is to act as the Bankers' Bank, supporting and supervising commercial banks and acting as their lender of last resort if they need more funds to avoid insolvency. The third is to liaise with the Central Banks of other sovereign nations in ensuring smooth convertibility of the national currency. Today, this final function is conducted within a framework of floating exchange rates.

Together, these three competences imply that the Central Bank has considerable influence over the growth of the money supply. How competently this influence has been exercised is a matter of debate examined in greater detail in Appendix 1.

The Jamaican Model

The Anglo-Saxon model is applied today in the USA, the UK and other advanced economies with mature banking systems and financial markets.

Under what might be termed the Jamaican model, as set out in Chapter 4, the role of the Central Bank in emerging economies extends beyond the Anglo-Saxon competences to include the creation of specialised financial institutions such as building societies, agricultural credit banks, and development finance companies able to lend for longer periods than commercial banks. It may also involve playing an active role in developing national securities markets and sponsoring and supervising national stock exchanges.

The Stability of the Financial System Matters

In both the Anglo-Saxon and Jamaican models, the Central Bank has a key role to play in ensuring the stability of the financial system. In the UK, the Bank of England was responsible for the regulation of the banking industry for most of the 20th century. However, following the failure of Barings Bank in 1995, responsibility for financial regulation was transferred to a new Financial Services Authority (FSA). The FSA's 'light touch' approach to financial regulation was deemed to have been one of the causes of the banking crises of 2007–2009 and it was wound up in 2013, after which regulatory authority was divided between the Financial Conduct Authority and the Bank of England. A simpler approach, particularly in emerging markets where regulatory expertise is scarce, would be to place responsibility firmly under the Central Bank.

What matters more than who regulates the financial system is how well it is regulated. The light touch approach adopted on both sides of the Atlantic in the run-up to the global financial crisis clearly failed, as banks aggressively leveraged up their equity bases with increasing amounts of debt, which was then used to fund loans at narrowing spreads to weak borrowers offering inadequate collateral.

In the USA, Alan Greenspan, Chairman of the Federal Reserve from 1987 to 2006, took a sanguine view of these developments. "I found the broad philosophy of unfettered market competition compelling, as I do to this day" he wrote in his autobiography, *The Age of Turbulence*, published on the very eve of the international financial crisis in September 2007. Eight years earlier, he had been an enthusiastic advocate of the American

Financial Services Modernisation Act, which, he wrote approvingly,

> *"finally did away with the Glass-Steagall Act, the Depression-era law that limited the ability of banks, investment firms and insurance companies to enter one another's markets...I agreed that liberalisation in these markets was long overdue."*[lxxi]

A year after the publication of *The Age Turbulence*, in testimony given to the US Congress in October 2008, the former Fed Chair had the grace to admit his error in supporting wholesale financial liberalisation. "I made a mistake in presuming that the self-interest of organisations, specifically banks and others, was such that they were best capable of protecting their own shareholders," he said.

In the aftermath of the financial crisis of 2007–2009, there were renewed efforts to separate commercial banks and building societies authorised to accept retail deposits on the one hand, from investment firms, private equity funds and venture capitalists not so authorised on the other.

As an absolute minimum, financial regulation should enforce clear separation of these two quite distinct functions. Regulatory standards need to be significantly higher for deposit-taking commercial banks than for investment companies that take more speculative positions funded by their shareholders rather than by customer deposits.

In my account of the causes of the banking collapses of 2007–2009, *The Golden Guinea*[lxxii], I analysed the accounts of Newcastle-based Northern Rock and the two leading Scottish banks, the Royal Bank of Scotland (RBS) and Halifax Bank of Scotland (HBOS), to find out what had gone wrong. The analysis identified seven signals that should have served as warning lights of trouble ahead:

1. *Rapid growth in the bank's loan portfolio*. In the case of Northern Rock, loans and advances more than doubled between 2003 and 2006.

2. *Diminished lending security*, with loans advanced on insufficient collateral. Northern Rock was one of the banks which, at the peak of the credit bubble, was reported to advance mortgages significantly greater than a property's independent valuation and to accept self-certification of a borrower's income as proof of ability to repay.

3. *Narrowing interest margins*. Northern Rock's spread between the interest earned and the interest paid by the bank, as reported in its Annual Accounts, fell from 1.55 per cent of its assets in 2003 to just 0.79 per cent in 2007.

4. *Falling administrative costs*, which had to be cut in order for the bank to survive on its declining net interest margin, but meant that detailed diligence checks were compromised.

5. *A declining equity base as a proportion of total assets*. In the case of Northern Rock, shareholders' funds as a proportion of its total assets fell from 3.6 per cent of gross assets at the end of 2003 to just

1.8 per cent at the end of 2006. A similar erosion of their equity base was evident in RBS and HBOS.

6. *Increased dependence on wholesale funding at the expense of customer deposits*. In the case of Northern Rock, wholesale funding rose from 35 per cent of gross assets in 2003 to 64 per cent by 2006. Although in principle customer deposits can be withdrawn on demand, they are, in practice, a reasonably stable source of bank funding because a bank has many thousands of customers, not all of whom will wish to withdraw their deposits at the same time. By contrast, wholesale funding provided by a few large lenders or borrowed on the overnight money market may be withdrawn at short notice.

7. *Declining liquid reserves*. The practice that prevailed for much of the 20th century, under which commercial banks retained approximately thirty per cent of their assets in cash or assets easily converted into cash, was a distant memory by 2007. By the end of 2007, Northern Rock's liquid assets were just seven per cent of its total assets, completely inadequate to meet large withdrawal requests.

The Fundamental Equation of Bank Solvency set out in Appendix 2 can be applied to any bank's accounts to analyse how sound it is and calculate the risk that it may run into financial trouble. A banking regulator – whether it be a division within a Central Bank or a separate organisation – should ensure that, as an absolute minimum, a commercial bank's equity falls to no less than 7½ per cent of its gross assets and its liquid assets fall to no less than twenty per cent of gross assets. Customer deposits should finance no less than sixty per cent of loans and advances. Finally, the net interest margin should be a minimum of 1½ per cent of a bank's loan portfolio to cover their administrative overheads and bad debt provisions.

All these ratios can be calculated from the audited accounts of commercial banks. The regulator should complement ratio analysis with sample checks to ensure that a bank is lending on adequate collateral and has proper procedures in place to confirm their borrowers' ability to service their loans on agreed terms.

These rules should help to safeguard, not only individual banks, but the wider stability of the banking system.

****

In enforcing these rules, banking regulators have similar sanctions at their disposal as football referees, which they can escalate as required to ensure compliance.

A light touch may be appropriate if all participants are playing fairly and safely. However, as Alan Greenspan, the most experienced central banker of his generation, discovered at the cost of his reputation, this cannot be taken as given.

The first sanction for a breach of the rules might be a word of warning – a chat with the team captain, or, in the case of a commercial bank, its Chair – suggesting that closer attention to the playing rules would be in order, accompanied by a word of warning about possible consequences if they are not. During the days of the 20th century British banking oligopoly, it was said that the Governor of the Bank of England merely had to raise an eyebrow to persuade a commercial bank's chairman to tighten up credit standards. After the credit explosion that led to the banking crisis of 2007–2009, and the inflationary spike of the early 2020s, perhaps it is time for the Governor to occasionally exercise his eyebrows once more.

If a friendly word does not suffice, the second sanction is a penalty; in the case of a bank, fines in proportion to the gravity of their offence. Fines could be reinforced by a requirement to deposit more of a bank's reserves at the Central Bank, thus automatically increasing its liquid assets.

If any player continues to breach the rules, the ultimate sanction is a sending off. In the past, Central Banks and Finance Ministries have played active roles in engineering the acquisition of weak banks teetering on the brink of insolvency by stronger banks, and dismissing the senior management of the weaker bank.

****

Individuals come and individuals go, but ideas, nations and families may endure indefinitely.

My father lived long enough to see me married (and happily well off his hands) and start a family of my own. I retain his published work, and much unpublished, in my own library, and it has proved more than useful over the years, not so much in the noble pursuit of academic truth, which was my father's mission, but in the rather less noble pursuit of monetary gain on the financial markets, where the analysis of the Swansea School has proved a most helpful guide. During the 1980s, I came across a book with the intriguing title *How to make $1,000,000 in the Stock Market – Automatically!* Inspired by this characteristically American brio, perhaps one day I will sit down to write *How to make $1 million in the Bond Market,* or some such title, relating how the principles of the Swansea School were appliedto that end. But that is another story.

A New Generation Arrives.

Jamie and I at home in London, 1989

Technical Appendices

Appendix 1 Money and Inflation

The Quantity Theory: A Rudimentary Exposition

What has been described as "the oldest of all economic theories" is not, in its original form, a predictive theory at all, but an accounting identity, which may be formally expressed as:

$$PT = MV \qquad [1]$$

where P = the average price per transaction,

T = the total number of transactions,

M = the quantity of money in the economy, and

V = the velocity of circulation, or rate at which the quantity of money circulates around the economy.

Equation [1], sometimes referred to as the Classical Quantity Theory, is true by definition. *PT* – the number of transactions multiplied by the average price per transaction – is equal to a country's nominal Gross Domestic Product (GDP), while the supply of money *M* multiplied by the rate at which it is spent *V* must also equate to nominal GDP.

Substituting nominal GDP for PT in Equation [1] gives:

$$GDP = MV \qquad [2]$$

The Monetarist School developed this equality into a predictive equation on the premise that *V*, the rate at which money is spent, is reasonably stable, and that changes in the quantity of money *M* drives subsequent changes in nominal GDP, or formally:

$$GDP_{t+1} = MV_t \qquad [3]$$

Two further premises of the Monetarist School are that:

- if an economy is operating at or close to full employment, *T*, the number of transactions, is reasonably constant, and
- the quantity of money, *M*, is under the ultimate control of the Central Bank.

If *V* and *T* are reasonably constant, then Equation [3] may be reformulated as

$$P_{t+1} = f(M_t) \qquad [4]$$

Equation [4] states that the price level in one period is a function, f, of the quantity of money in the previous period. Therefore, if a government wishes to bring down the rate of price inflation, it must first reduce the rate of monetary growth.

The Evidence

In practice, attempts to control inflation by means of monetary targets have met with mixed results. For example, during the 1980s, the British Government adopted a policy of monetary targeting and raised the Base Rate to more than 15 per cent in 1981 in an effort to restrain credit growth. The rate of inflation did indeed decline, but only at the cost of a severe recession. Unemployment rose to more than three million, while the relationship between monetary growth and the subsequent rate of inflation proved not to be stable and predictable in the way indicated by Equation [4]. This led critics of the Monetarist School to conclude that the velocity of circulation of money is not stable, because it is not possible to define exactly what money is. Although it is easy to define what money *does* – serving as a means of exchange, store of value, and unit of account – it is difficult to specify exactly what it comprises. Cigarettes, seashells, gold and digital constructs like Bitcoin have all been accepted as methods of payment at different times in different places. Many major corporate acquisitions are financed by shares issued by the acquiring company to pay shareholders of the acquired company, so a company's shares can serve as its currency, as the financier Jim Slater, Chairman of Slater Walker, explained in his memoir *Return to Go*[lxxiii]. During the Jacobite Rising of 1745, promissory notes signed by John Roy Stuart, Colonel of the Edinburgh Regiment, were accepted in payment for food to supply his starving soldiers. And so forth. In short, money is a *will o'the wisp* impossible to pin down.

Given the chameleon-like character of money, critics of Monetarism argue that it is not possible for a Central Bank to control its supply. Goodhart's Law[lxxiv] states that "when a monetary measure becomes a target, it ceases to be a good measure," because new forms of money are devised that fall outside the scope of any target a government or Central Bank may choose to employ.

Whilst these objections lead one to conclude that the strong version of the Quantity Theory, as set out in Equation [4], does not hold, a weaker version following from Equation [3] may still be valid as a basis for monetary policy, provided that *V*, the rate at which money circulates around the economy, is sufficiently stable in relation to the supply of money, however defined.

From Equation [2], *V* is defined as *GDP / M*. Data from the first half of the twentieth century, from 1900 to 1949, is presented in Figure A1.1, using M2 or 'narrow' money, comprising cash and current bank accounts, as the proxy for money supply.

Figure A1.1:
The velocity of circulation of money in the United Kingdom, 1900-1949 [GDP/M2]

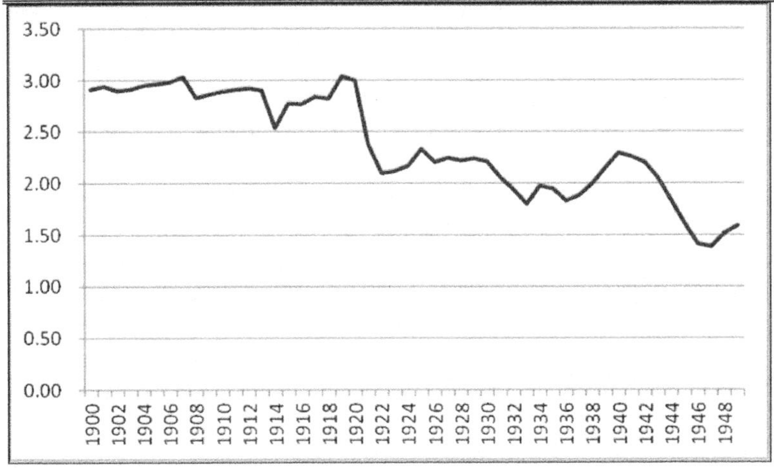

Source: Adapted from data in Edward Nevin and E.W. Davis, *The London Clearing Banks*, Elek, London, 1970: Table 1, pp 290 - 293 for GNP at factor cost and Money Supply during the period 1900-1949.

Figure A1.1 shows that *V* fell by approximately a half, from 3.0 to 1.5, over the entire time period. However, it does appear to have been reasonably stable over shorter time intervals such as 1900-1918 and during the interwar years. This short-term stability, together with the experience of the inflationary impact of rapid monetary growth during the First World War, convinced the British authorities during the Second World War that they needed to keep the growth of money supply under tight control. Whereas UK prices were two and a half times higher in 1920 than they had been in 1914, they were only a third higher in 1945 compared to 1940 – still a significant increase, but considerably less than in the earlier war.

Figure A1.2 graphs the rate of inflation in the UK in the century and a quarter between 1900 and 2023. It shows four major inflationary spikes during that period: during the First World War, the Second World War, the 1970s, and the early 2020s. Each of these spikes was associated with a significant increase in the UK's money supply. The wartime spikes were driven by increases in military expenditure not fully funded by taxation, savings or overseas borrowing. The spike during the 1970s was driven by American Balance of Payments deficits, which resulted in a significant increase in UK money supply. Under the Bretton Woods regime, the UK and other trading partners of the United States had to convert dollars into their own currencies at fixed exchange rates, resulting in an increase in money supply beyond their control because:

$$M = C + F \qquad [5]$$

where C = domestically created currency and credit, and

F = currency and credit created by foreign exchange transactions under a fixed exchange rate system.[lxxv]

Figure A1.2:
The rate of inflation in the UK, 1900-2023

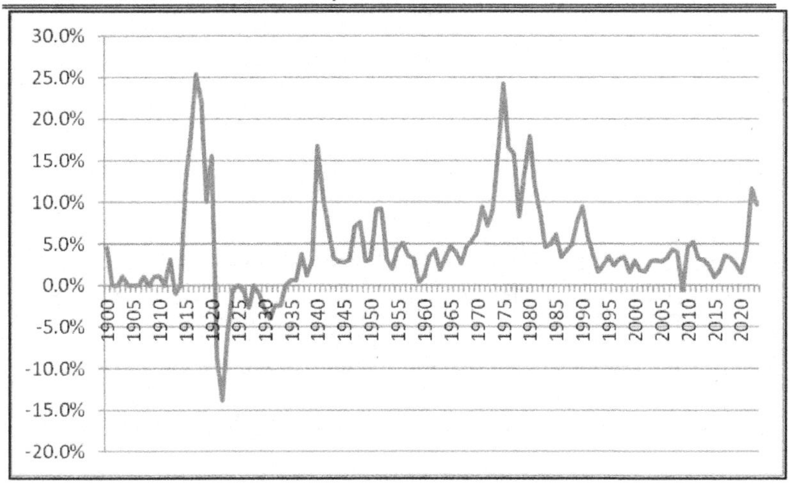

Source: Office of National Statistics, Retail Prices Index

It is perhaps too early at the time of writing to arrive at any final conclusions regarding the causes of the fourth inflationary spike during the early 2020s. However, some provisional observations can be made.

The first is that the velocity of circulation of money does not appear to have been stable during the early years of the 21st century but to have steadily declined, as shown in Figure A1.3. This figure uses Sterling M3 as the proxy for money supply. M3 is a broader measure of money than M2, covering not only cash and money held in customers' current bank accounts, as does M2, but also bank deposits that can only be withdrawn after a specified time period not included in M2.

Figure A1.3 shows that the velocity of circulation of M3 fell by more than a half between 2001 and 2009 before stabilising between 2010 and 2019. It then experienced a further downward lurch in 2020.

Figure A1.3:
The velocity of circulation of money in the United Kingdom, 2001-2023 [GDP/M3]

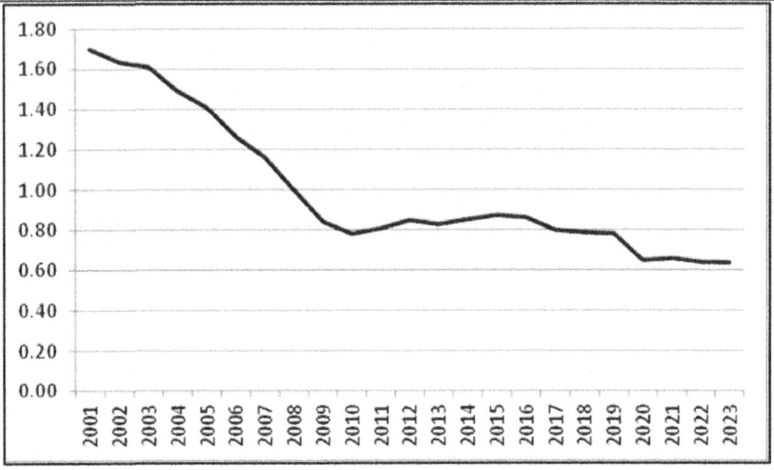

Sources: [1] ONS, Dataset ID PN2, Release date 15-02-2024 for GDP. [2] The Bank of England for M3 seasonally adjusted, Series LPQVWYZ

It is possible that the decline in the first decade of the 21st century was a manifestation of Goodhart's Law. As new forms of money and credit developed, the importance of M3 as a means of exchange diminished, while the importance of forms of personal and household credit not included in M3 increased.[lxxvi]

The main factor in the decline in the velocity of circulation of M3 in 2020 was the Covid-19 lockdown, which restricted the expenditure of both individuals and companies.

Whatever the cause, the decline in *V* over the period reinforced the view that changes in money supply were not reliable predictors of changes in the subsequent rate of inflation. However, Monetarism continued to have powerful advocates. In a letter to the *Financial Times* on November 7th 2023[lxxvii], eight leading economists expressed their concern about the damaging effects of fluctuations in monetary growth.

> *"In April 2021 we signed a letter to you warning that the then rapid growth of the quantity of money — of more than 15 per cent in the previous 12 months — would result in well above-target inflation. The position today is very different. In the year to September 2023 the quantity of money fell by 4.2 per cent. By 'the quantity of money' we mean the M4x aggregate prepared by the Bank of England. The 4.2 per cent fall is the largest to have been recorded in twenty-six years of data. Indeed, until 2023 no annual decline in this measure of money had occurred at all, not even in the Great Recession of 2008 and 2009."*

The letter went on to warn that the fall in money supply could lead to below target inflation or even deflation in 2025 or 2026, and concluded by criticising the Bank of England for ignoring the rate of monetary growth.

> *"Large fluctuations in money growth are a menace to the British economy. In our view the Bank of England is again mismanaging monetary policy. Lurches in only a few years from much above target inflation to deflation are destructive and unnecessary, and can have tragic consequences for households and companies. We recommend stability in money growth at a low rate. Stability in money growth should prevent big swings in demand, output and employment, while an appropriately low increase in money contributes to on-target inflation."*

Although the eight signatories to the November 2023 letter use M4x as their measure of money supply, the same trends are evident in M3, as shown in Figure A1.4. The figure shows that M3 grew rapidly in the run-up to the global financial crisis of 2007-09 before falling sharply in its aftermath. The fall reflected severe credit contraction after the collapse of several major banks. In response, the Bank of England, along with other leading Central Banks including the American Federal Reserve and the European Central Bank, cut the rate of interest at which they lent to commercial banks to the lowest rate in history – just 0.5 per cent in the case of the Bank of England, which reduced its

Base Rate even further to 0.1 per cent during the 2020/21 Covid pandemic.

Interest rates remained at these historically unprecedented lows despite high rates of monetary growth. In the case of the UK, M3 increased by twenty-four per cent between December 2021 and December 2023. If the rate of real GDP is approximately one per cent a year, as it has been since 1990, then the high rate of monetary growth experienced in 2022 and 2023 is likely to generate inflation well in excess of the Bank of England's CPI target of two per cent per year.

Figure A1:4:
Annual Percentage Growth in M3 and the UK Base Rate, 2002-2023

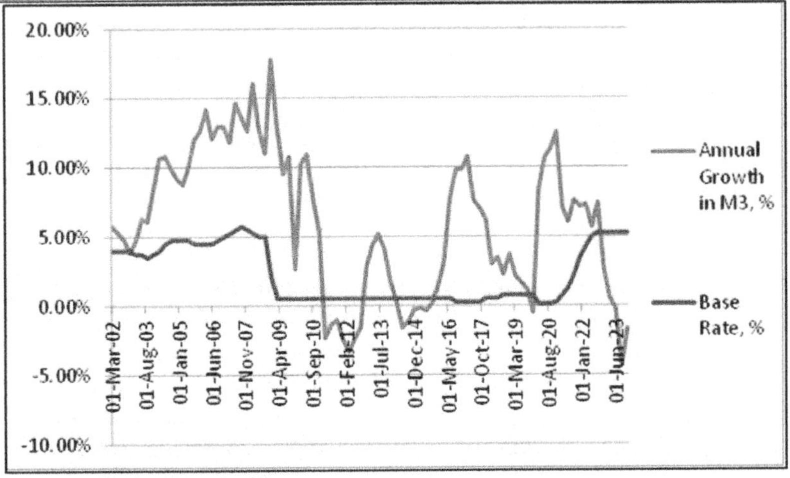

Source: Bank of England

Future Outlook

At the time of writing, in mid-2024, the forecasts of Juan Castañeda, Tim Congdon *et al* in their November 2023 *Financial Times* letter, of rapidly falling inflation in 2024, have to date been borne out. British monetary history since 1900 does seem to support the general principle enunciated by Milton Friedman, that "inflation is always and everywhere a monetary phenomenon."

Given the difficulties of precisely defining what money is, the Bank of England should monitor a series of monetary aggregates, seeking to keep their growth to an absolute maximum of six per cent a year. Changes in the Base Rate are one method of achieving this target, but the Bank of England has other tools that it can deploy. For example, it could vary the level of reserves that regulated financial institutions are required to hold at the Bank, or use its own open market operations to mop up surplus liquidity by issuing more gilt-edged stock and Treasury Bills than needed to fund the Government's own requirements. It could even apply the technique reported to have been deployed during the 20th century, of using the persuasive powers of the Governor of the Bank of England to persuade the chairmen of commercial banks to tighten their lending criteria if required to rein back domestic credit creation.

Appendix 2 A Model of Financial Intermediation[lxxviii]

Note: *In this Appendix, 'loan' is used as a generic term to cover both loan and equity investments, and 'loan portfolio' includes shares and other securities in the portfolio of a financial intermediary.*

The Fundamental Equation of Bank Solvency

Any financial intermediary must make a return on its loans at least equal to the costs it incurs to finance them. If it fails to do so, it will sustain losses, and ultimately, when its reserves are exhausted, go out of operation. Formally, in order for a financial intermediary to survive, it must be the case that:

$$(1 - p)\,(1 + r) >= 1 + a + i \qquad [1]$$

where:

r = the percentage return on the financial intermediary's loan portfolio. This is computed as its annual income from interest on the loans it advances, plus annual dividends and capital gains earned on its equity investments, divided by the total value of its portfolio;

i = the average percentage cost of capital raised to finance the portfolio;

a = annual average administrative costs as a percentage of the total portfolio;

p = annual probability of default as a percentage of the portfolio. This is calculated as: the annual value of bad debts and write-downs of equity investments, *plus*, in the case of any intermediary trading in more than one currency, any foreign exchange gains or *less* any foreign exchange losses, divided by the total value of its loan portfolio.

The left-hand side of the Equation [1] expresses the return per monetary unit (say US dollar) of a financial institution's portfolio, while the right-hand side expresses the cost per dollar raised to finance the portfolio.

As a minimum, in order to remain solvent, a financial intermediary must at least break even on its loan operations. For this condition to be met, Equation [1] becomes an equality:

$$(1 - p)\,(1 + r) = 1 + a + i \qquad [2]$$

Multiplying out gives:

$$1 - p + r - pr = 1 + a + i \quad [3]$$

Subtracting 1 and adding p to each side of Equation [3] gives:

$$r - pr = a + i + p \quad [4]$$

Gathering terms:

$$r\,(1 - p) = a + i + p \quad [5]$$

The Fundamental Equation of Bank Solvency can be derived from Equation [5] by dividing through by (1 – p), which gives:

$$\mathbf{r = \frac{a + i + p}{(1 - p)}} \quad \mathbf{[6]}$$

Equation [6] states that, in order to remain solvent, a financial intermediary must earn a return on its total portfolio at least equal to the costs it incurs on raising and investing the funds to finance the portfolio (*a + i*) less the probability of default (*p*), divided by a factor equal to 1 minus the probability of default (*1 – p*).

Default Probabilities and Bank Solvency

One implication of the Fundamental Equation of Bank Solvency is that a financial intermediary needs to pay close attention to the probability of default on its portfolio (*p* in Equation [6]). The reason is that any given percentage increase in the probability of default will cause the required return, *r*, to increase by *more* than that percentage, since an increase in the probability of default increases the value of the numerator in Equation [6] and simultaneously reduces the value of the denominator.

However, while a financial intermediary can budget for every other variable in Equation [6], it cannot precisely forecast the annual probability of default, including any foreign exchange losses that it may suffer as a consequence of currency fluctuations, which are beyond its direct control.

Makhtar Diop, Managing Director of the International Finance Corporation (IFC), cited a March 2024 report by the Global Emerging Markets Risk Data Consortium (GEM)[lxxix] of twenty-five multilateral development banks, which reported a default rate of companies to which GEM institutions advanced loans between 1994 and 2022 of approximately 3½ per cent per annum.

If p = 3½ per cent in line with the GEM default rate, a = 4.0% which was the average administrative cost in twenty-five national Development Finance Companies (DFCs) to which the European Investment Bank (EIB) lent under the first two Lomé Conventions between 1976 and 1986[lxxx], and i = 3.0%, the rate at which the EIB lent Euros to national DFCs under its Global Loan operations, then substituting into Equation [6] would gives

$$r = \frac{i + a + p}{(1 - p)} = \frac{3\% + 4\% + 3.5\%}{(1 - 3.5\%)} = 10.88\% \qquad [7]$$

The calculations in Equation [7] imply that a national DFC would need to on-lend at rates of at least eleven per cent in order to break even, and that its on-lending spread ($r - i$) would need to be at least eight per cent.

The EIB limited the on-lending spread that a DFC could charge to between four and eight per cent under the first two Lomé Conventions.[lxxxi] The analysis in this Appendix suggests that this was unlikely be sufficient for a DFC to earn a sufficient margin to enable it to break even. Moreover, as many DFCs lent to companies in their national currencies, but borrowed from the EIB in ECU (forerunner of the Euro), they were exposed to foreign exchange losses if their national currency was devalued, increasing the risk of insolvency. The restrictions that the EIB placed upon DFCs in an effort to ensure that their borrowers would gain the benefit of the low interest rates therefore risked undermining the solvency of the DFCs themselves.

Administrative Costs and Loan Values

The EIB and other multilateral development banks need viable DFCs if they are to reach small- and medium-sized enterprises (SMEs), because loan appraisal and monitoring costs are too high for the multilaterals to lend directly to SMEs.

Rearranging Equation [7] to derive p gives:

$$p = \frac{(r - i)}{(1 + r)} - \frac{a}{(1 + r)} \qquad [8]$$

Differentiating *p* with respect to *a* gives:

$$\frac{\delta p}{\delta a} = \frac{1}{(1 + r)} \quad [9]$$

Equation [9] defines the extent to which the probability of default needs to be reduced for any increase in proportionate administrative costs to be justified, given the values of *r* and *i*.

Equation [9] gives rise to the following conclusions:

- the average cost of funds, *i*, is irrelevant in determining the extent to which bad debts have to be reduced for any increase in administrative overheads to be justified;
- the sole determinant is the required return on the portfolio, *r*;
- the lower the return a financial intermediary earns on its loan portfolio, the greater the reduction in bad debts needs to be for any increase in administrative costs to be justified, because $\delta p/\delta a$ is inversely related to *r*.

The administrative costs of a financial intermediary comprise three components:

- the costs of raising and managing the funds required to finance its loan portfolio;
- the costs of appraising new loans; and
- the costs of managing and monitoring existing loans.

This may help to explain why, as described in Chapter 7 and more extensively in *The Golden Guinea*, the administrative costs of banks which collapsed during the financial crisis of 2007–2009 had fallen as a proportion of their loan portfolios during the preceding years, compromising their loan appraisals at a time when the banks should have been tightening their lending criteria. The lower lending rates that they were offering in an effort to increase their market share forced the banks to reduce their administrative overheads to remain profitable. However, this proved to be a false economy.

Formally, a bank's administrative costs may be expressed as follows:

$$AC_t = F_t + c(Q_t) + d\,(n_t) + g(N_t) \quad [10]$$

where:

AC_t = the total Administrative Costs of a financial intermediary during time period t;

F_t = the fixed overhead costs of the financial intermediary during period t, independent of the number or value of loans made by it;

Q_t = the total value of the intermediary's loan portfolio at the beginning of period t;

n_t = the number of new loans signed during period t; and

N_t = the total number of loans on the intermediary's Balance Sheet at the beginning of period t;

and c', d' and g' are all positive (>0) – i.e., an intermediary's administrative costs will be greater:

- the higher its Fixed Cost base *F*,
- the greater the value of its loan portfolio *Q*,
- the more new loan agreements it enters into during the period under consideration *n*, and
- the greater the total number of loans it manages *N*.

Equation [10] may be simplified if n_t, the number of new loans signed during any year, is constant in relation to N_t, the total number of loans in a development bank's portfolio at the beginning of the year. If the relationship is stable, then Equation [10] may be simplified to:

$$AC_t = F_t + c(Q_t) + ß(N_t) \qquad [11]$$

where ß' >0. Dividing Equation [11] through by Q gives:

$$AC/Q = F/Q + ß\,(N/Q) + c \qquad [12]$$

AC/Q is equal to *a*, the proportionate administrative overheads of a financial intermediary in the Fundamental Equation of Bank Solvency (Equation [6]), while *N/Q* may be written as *1/X*, where *X* is the average value of a loan within the financial intermediary's portfolio (*X* = *Q/N*). The other variables in Equation [12], *F/Q* and *c*, are fixed in value, and may be represented by the Greek letter alpha or *α*, so *(F/Q + c) = α*.

Substituting these expressions into Equation [12] gives:

$$a = \alpha + ß(1/X) \qquad `[13]$$

If ß is a power function, Equation [13] becomes

$a = \alpha + X^{\beta}$ [14]

This was the relationship tested in the *Savings and Development* paper[lxxxii] which reviewed the accounts of nineteen international development banks as follows:

- the three institutions of the World Bank Group: the International Development Association (IDA), the main International Bank for Reconstruction and Development (IBRD), and the International Finance Corporation (IFC);
- five members of the Interact Group of European development banks: CDC, DEG, FMO, IFU and SBI;
- five regional development banks: the African Development Bank (AfDB), the Asian Development Bank (ADB), the Inter-American Development Bank (IDB), the Islamic Development Bank (IsDB) and the Arab Bank for Economic Development in Africa (BADEA);
- the soft loan arms of three of these banks – the African Development Fund (AfDF), the Asian Development Fund (ADF), the Inter-American Development Fund (IDF), and
- three private sector development banks, CDFC, EDESA and SIFIDA.

The results are shown in Figure A2.1. The vertical axis of the figure measures the administrative overheads of each of the nineteen international development banks in the sample as a proportion of their portfolio value (*a*), while the horizontal axis measures their average loan size (*X*) in US $ million. The data is derived from the Annual Accounts of each bank in 1981/82.

Figure A2.1 shows that there was an inverse power relationship between the average size of loans made by the nineteen banks in the sample and their administrative overheads, as given in Equation [14]:

$$a = \alpha + X^{\beta}$$

where` α, the estimated intercept parameter = 4.33

β, the estimated slope parameter = - 0.5, and

R^2, the estimated correlation coefficient = 0.88.

The relationship shown in the graph indicates that, in the early 1980s, substantial economies were reaped by development banks as they increased their lending operations up to approximately US$5 million, but thereafter there was more limited scope for further economies by spreading administrative overheads over a larger average loan size.

The conclusion in the mid-1980s was that, in order to keep the cost of lending manageable, multilateral development banks needed to lend a minimum of approximately $5 million in any single loan operation. Adjusted for inflation, this would indicate a minimum viable loan size of between $15 and $20 million for multilateral development banks in the mid-2020s. The minimum amount could be computed more accurately by replicating the 1985 analysis.

Figure A2.1:
The relationship between percentage administrative overheads and average loan size of 19 international development banks in 1981/82

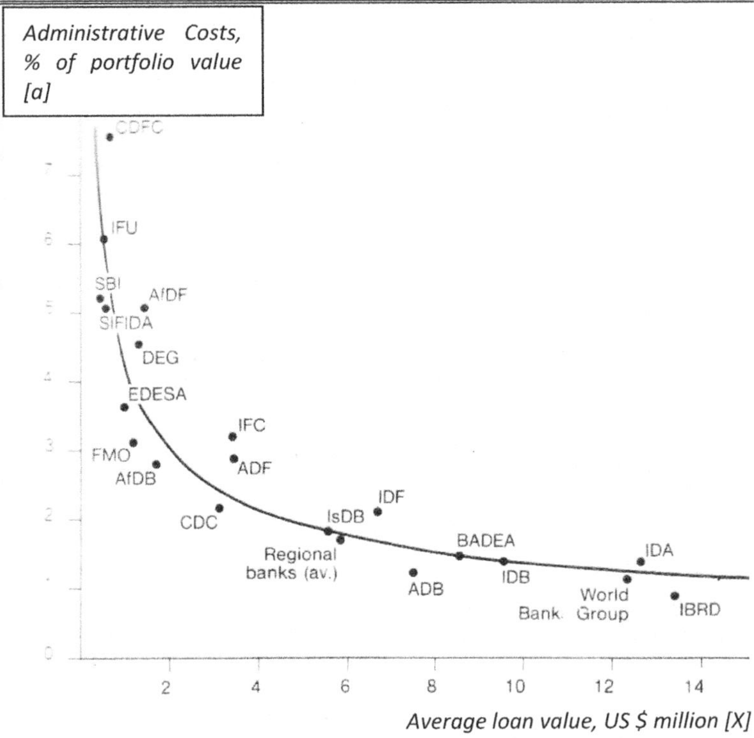

Source: Reproduced from M. Nevin, 'Dilemmas in Development Banking', *Savings and Development*, No 4, 1985 IX, p 423

References

[i] As evidenced in David Lough, *No More Champagne: Churchill and his Money*, Head of Zeus, 2015
[ii] J.M. Keynes, *The Economic Consequences of Mr Churchill*, Hogarth Press, London, 1925
[iii] Edward Nevin, *Diary of a Lifetime*, unpublished family memoir, 1983
[iv] Edward Nevin, *Diary of a Lifetime*, 1983, pp 10-11
[v] Edward Nevin, *Diary of a Lifetime*, 1983
[vi] Edward Nevin, *Diary of a Lifetime*, 1983, p. 17
[vii] R.F. Kahn, 'The Relation of Home Investment to Unemployment,' *Economic Journal*, No 41, 1931, pp 173-198
[viii] Sylvia Nasar, *Grand Pursuit: A Story of Economic Genius: Great 20th Century Economic Thinkers and What They Discovered About the Way the World Works,* Fourth Estate, 2011
[ix]Edward Nevin, *The Mechanism of Cheap Money*, University of Wales Press, 1955, p. vii
[x] Nahid Aslanbeigui and Guy Oakes, *The Provocative Joan Robinson: The Making of a Cambridge Economist*, Duke University Press, Durham & London, 2009
[xi] *New York Times* obituary of Joan Robinson, August 11th 1983
[xii] J.M. Keynes, *The General Theory of Employment, Interest and Money*, Palgrave Macmillan, 1936
[xiii] Quoted in Edward Nevin, *Waiting for Godot*, inaugural lecture at the University College of Swansea, 1969
[xiv] Edward Nevin, *The Mechanism of Cheap Money*, University of Wales Press, 1955, p. 76
[xv] Edward Nevin, *The Mechanism of Cheap Money*, University of Wales Press, 1955, p. 94
[xvi] Quoted in Edward Nevin, *The Mechanism of Cheap Money*, University of Wales Press, 1955, p. 99
[xvii] Michael Nevin, 'Welsh academic's lesson from history suggest austerity will follows Darling', Western Mail, April 15th 2009
[xviii] John Maynard Keynes, *How to pay for the war: a radical plan for the Chancellor of the Exchequer*. Macmillan & Co, London, 1940
[xix] Edward Nevin, *The Market in Gilt-Edged Securities, September 1939-December 1949*, A dissertation submitted for the degree of Master of Arts of the University of Wales, September 1950

[xx] Edward Nevin and E.W. Davis, *The London Clearing Banks*, 1970, Table 1, pp 292-293. 'Money supply' in this table is defined as currency in circulation plus net deposits at the London Clearing Banks.
[xxi] Edward Nevin, *The Market in Gilt-Edged Securities, September 1939-December 1949*, p. 64
[xxii] Edward Nevin, *The Market in Gilt-Edged Securities, September 1939-December 1949*, pp. 66-67
[xxiii] Obituary of Professor E. T. Nevin by Professor George Clayton, *Independent*, London, September 21st 1992
[xxiv] Edward Nevin, *The Market in Gilt-Edged Securities, September 1939-December 1949*, p. 71
[xxv] Edward Nevin, *The Market in Gilt-Edged Securities, September 1939-December 1949*, p. 188
[xxvi] A.H. Halsey (ed), *Trends in British Society since 1900*, Macmillan, 1972, Table 4.11, p. 122, The Cost of Living Index in the UK, 1900-1968
[xxvii] Edward Nevin, *Diary of a Lifetime*, 1983 (unpublished), p.26
[xxviii] Edward Nevin, *Diary of a Lifetime*, 1983, pp.26-27
[xxix] Edward Nevin, *Diary of a Lifetime*, 1983, p.28
[xxx] Edward Nevin, *The Problem of the National Debt*, University of Wales Press, 1954, pp. 10-11
[xxxi] Edward Nevin, *The Problem of the National Debt*, University of Wales Press, 1954, p. 56
[xxxii] https://www.dmo.gov.uk/data/pdfdatareport?reportCode=D1A
[xxxiii] https://obr.uk/forecasts-in-depth/tax-by-tax-spend-by-spend/debt-interest-central-government-net/
[xxxiv] Edward Nevin, *The Problem of the National Debt*, University of Wales Press, 1954, p.108
[xxxv] Edward Nevin, *Diary of a Lifetime*, 1983, unpublished, p.29
[xxxvi] Edward Nevin, *Diary of a Lifetime*, 1983, unpublished, p.32
[xxxvii] Edward Nevin, *Diary of a Lifetime*, 1983, p.33
[xxxviii] Edward Nevin, *Diary of a Lifetime*, 1983, p.34
[xxxix] Quoted in Sean Martin Enright, *William Nevin, 575th Mayor of Pembroke*, 2021
[xl] Quoted in Sean Martin Enright, *William Nevin 575th Mayor of Pembroke*, 2021
[xli] Edward Nevin, *Diary of a Lifetime*, 1983, p.42
[xlii] Edward Nevin, *Diary of a Lifetime*, 1983, pp.42-43
[xliii] Edward Nevin, *Diary of a Lifetime*, 1983, p.47
[xliv] Edward Nevin, *Diary of a Lifetime*, 1983, p.48
[xlv] Edward Nevin, *Capital Funds in Underdeveloped Countries: The Role of Financial Institutions*, Macmillan & Co, London, 1963

[xlvi] Edward Nevin, *Capital Funds in Underdeveloped Countries: The Role of Financial Institutions*, Macmillan & Co, London, 1963, p. vii
[xlvii] Edward Nevin, *Capital Funds in Underdeveloped Countries: The Role of Financial Institutions*, Macmillan & Co, London, 1963, pp 46-47
[xlviii] Edward Nevin, *Capital Funds in Underdeveloped Countries: The Role of Financial Institutions*, Macmillan & Co, London, 1963, p 51
[xlix] Edward Nevin, *Capital Funds in Underdeveloped Countries: The Role of Financial Institutions*, Macmillan & Co, London, 1963, p 55.
[l] Edward Nevin, *Capital Funds in Underdeveloped Countries: The Role of Financial Institutions*, Macmillan & Co, London, 1963, p 72.
[li] Edward Nevin, *Capital Funds in Underdeveloped Countries: The Role of Financial Institutions*, Macmillan & Co, London, 1963, p 75.
[lii] Michael Nevin, 'The European Investment Bank and African development companies', in Jeffery I. Round (ed), *The European Economy in Perspective: Essays in Honour of Edward Nevin*, Cardiff, University of Wales Press, pp 245- 265
[liii] Edward Nevin, *Capital Funds in Underdeveloped Countries: The Role of Financial Institutions*, Macmillan & Co, London, 1963, p 87
[liv] The Obituary Notice is reproduced in Sean Martin Enright, *William Nevin 575th Mayor of Pembroke*, 2021
[lv] J.R. Hicks, 'Mr Keynes and the Classics', *Econometrica,* April 1937
[lvi] Edward Nevin, A.R. Roe, and J.I. Round, *The Structure of the Welsh Economy*, Cardiff, University of Wales Press, 1966
[lvii] Edward Nevin and E.W. Davis, *The London Clearing Banks*, London, Elek Books, 1970. Table 6, p.203.
[lviii] Michael Nevin, *The Age of Illusions: The Political Economy of Britain, 1968-1982*, London, Victor Gollancz, 1983
[lix] Michael Nevin, 'How we lost a Golden Age', *Western Mail,* March 5th 1985
[lx] Michael Nevin, 'How we lost a Golden Age', *Western Mail,* March 5th 1985
[lxi] Edward Nevin, *Economics: Waiting for Godot*. Inaugural Lecture of the Professor of Economics delivered at the College on February 25th 1969, University College of Swansea, 1969
[lxii] Edward Nevin, *Economics: Waiting for Godot.*, University College of Swansea, 1969, p.9
[lxiii] Edward Nevin, *Economics: Waiting for Godot.*, University College of Swansea, 1969, p.15
[lxiv] Edward Nevin, *Economics: Waiting for Godot.*, University College of Swansea, 1969, p.17

[lxv] Edward Nevin, 'Miners' battle against destiny is one they cannot win', *Western Mail*, January 20th 1972

[lxvi] Edward Nevin, 'The price of coal could be your lost job', *Western Mail*, February 15th 1972

[lxvii] Edward Nevin, *Economics: Waiting for Godot.*, University College of Swansea, 1969, p.24

[lxviii] Edward Nevin, *The Pay of the Policeman*, Police Federation of England and Wales, London, 1975

[lxix] Edward Nevin, *The Pay of the Policeman*, A Report for the Police Federation, 1975, p. 8, para 20

[lxx] Edward Nevin, *The Economics of Europe*, Macmillan, London, 1990

[lxxi] Alan Greenspan, *The Age of Turbulence: Adventures in a New World*, The Penguin Press, New York, 2007, Chapter 9

[lxxii] Michael Nevin, *The Golden Guinea: The International Financial Crisis – Causes, Consequences and Cures*, Southdown Books, London, 2012

[lxxiii] Jim Slater, *Return to Go*, Weidenfeld & Nicolson, London, 1977

[lxxiv] Charles Goodhart, 'Problems of Monetary Management: The U.K. Experience', *Papers in Monetary Economics*, pp. 1-20. Vol. 1. Reserve Bank of Australia, Sydney, 1975

[lxxv] Harry G. Johnson, 'The Monetary Approach to Balance-of-Payments Theory', in *Further Essays in Monetary Economics (Collected Works of Harry Johnson)*, Routledge, London, 1972

[lxxvi] https://themoneycharity.org.uk/media/April-2024-Money-Statistics.pdf

[lxxvii] Juan Castañeda, Tim Congdon et al, 'Lurches in money supply are proven British menace', *Financial Times*, London, November 7th 2023

[lxxviii] Michael Nevin, 'Dilemmas in Development Banking', *Savings and Development*, Finafrica, Milan, Vol 4, 1985, pp 433-436

[lxxix] Makhtar Diop, 'Better risk data will help improve confidence in emerging markets', *Financial Times*, April 24th 2024

[lxxx] Michael Nevin, 'The European Investment Bank and African development companies', in Jeffery I. Round (ed), *The European Economy in Perspective: Essays in Honour of Edward Nevin*, Cardiff, University of Wales Press, Table 3, p. 260

[lxxxi] Michael Nevin, 'The European Investment Bank and African development companies', in Jeffery I. Round (ed), *The European Economy in Perspective: Essays in Honour of Edward Nevin*, Cardiff, University of Wales Press, p. 252

[lxxxii] Michael Nevin, 'Dilemmas in Development Banking', *Savings and Development*, Milan, Italy, No 4, 1985 IX, pp 421-438

Made in the USA
Monee, IL
05 November 2026

68006394R00094